BUILDING PROFESSIONAL
PRIDE IN LITERACY

The Professional Practices in Adult Education and Lifelong Learning Series explores issues and concerns of practitioners who work in the broad range of settings in adult and continuing education and lifelong learning.

The books provide information and strategies on how to make practice more effective for professionals and those they serve. They are written from a practical viewpoint and provide a forum for instructors, administrators, policy makers, counselors, trainers, instructional designers, and other related professionals. The series contains single author or coauthored books only and does not include edited volumes.

Sharan B. Merriam
Ronald M. Cervero
Series Editors

BUILDING PROFESSIONAL PRIDE IN LITERACY

A Dialogical Guide to Professional
Development for Practitioners of
Adult Literacy and Basic Education

[Benjamin]

B. Allan Quigley, EdD
St. Francis Xavier University

KRIEGER PUBLISHING COMPANY
MALABAR, FLORIDA
2006

Original Edition 2006

Printed and Published by
KRIEGER PUBLISHING COMPANY
KRIEGER DRIVE
MALABAR, FLORIDA 32950

Library of Congress Cataloging-in-Publication Data

Quigley, B. Allan (Benjamin Allan)
    Building professional pride in literacy : a dialogical guide to
professional development for practitioners of adult literacy and basic
education / B. Allan Quigley. — Original ed.
        p.   cm. — (Professional practices in adult education and lifelong
        learning series)
    Includes bibliographical references (p.) and index.
    ISBN 1-57524-262-1 (alk. paper)
        1. Adult education teachers—Training of. 2. Functional literacy.
    3. Basic education of adults. I. Title.

    LC5225.T4Q54 2006
    374'.0124—dc22   2006040836

10   9   8   7   6   5   4   3   2

Before this book went to press, a number of literacy practitioners at the Literacy Alliance of Greater New Orleans were in the midst of pilot testing the ideas in it. Then Hurricane Katrina hit. Despite the devastation that ensued, they regrouped and completed their discussions. This book is dedicated to the courage of those teachers and so many like them in the literacy field.
As well, it is for Patrick and Linda, and written in the memory of John Niemi.

CONTENTS

PREFACE

HOW TO MAKE BEST USE OF THIS GUIDE

Although adult educators from many areas of practice will find this guide useful, it was written with adult literacy and adult basic education (ABE) practitioners in mind. Teachers, tutors, administrators, counselors, and those in the many adult literacy support roles who are relatively new to the field are considered the main audience. More seasoned practitioners will not only benefit from this guide, but it is hoped they will share their knowledge with those newer to the field through the dialogical process outlined. Teachers of second languages—such as English as a Second Language (ESL) and French as a Second Language (FSL)—will also find this guide helpful. Adult education researchers, policy-makers, and anyone interested in the practice of adult literacy may well find the content of interest.

This guide seeks to initiate personal and group reflectio which, in turn, leads to activities and change. It is not intended to be a text that tries to "deposit expert knowledge" with readers—like the "banking" approach to education that Paolo Freire criticized years ago. Rather, this guide begins and ends by taking the position that no one has the monopoly on being an expert in education. Everyone has expertise. The view taken here is that we need to "make spaces where alternative ways of thinking and being can be worked up" (p. 82). In so doing, we can create the "knowledge . . . that is useful to those who generate it" (Barr, 1999, p. 82). This guide is dialogical in its design in order to help make such spaces and help make knowledge useful to those who are part of creating it.

As the author, I have tried to write in what I hope is a conversational style that is accessible and welcoming. And, I have had a lot of help in this from others, including those acknowledged earlier. My hope is that this style and format will encourage you to enter a dialogue on two levels. First, to write your reactions and reflections in a *learning journal* as we move through this guide (details on how this might be done are discussed later in this guide). And, second, to discuss those journal reflections, and other thoughts you will no doubt have, with those in your program, or those who are familiar with your program. These will be called your *co-learners*. They could include other adult education teachers, tutors, administrators, and those allied with your program, but they may well include your students as well.

However, many adult literacy and basic education practitioners will not be within the geographic vicinity of other practitioners and won't be able to meet regularly. Or, you may prefer not to meet with a group and may be more comfortable talking with only one or two others as your co-learners. Both scenarios are fine and are discussed in greater detail in a moment, but *dialogue, reflection, and action* are the keys to this guide, and they will need you to involve others.

As most will agree, we really do not spend enough time sharing our classroom concerns, our fears, our successes, our knowledge, or our trials with each other in adult education. Discussions are all too often on the weather, sports, politics, and those many systemic annoyances and issues in literacy and ABE programs, but there is a lonely isolationism to this. So, it is hoped this book will help *guide* you and your co-learners together into a new set of topics and activities that are stimulating, challenging, relevant to your work, all within a new space of dialogue that is safe for everyone involved. Finally, this guide is designed to give you and others some ways to assess and measure professional and program growth within the context of your classroom and your practice.

So, regardless of whether you are a part-time, full-time, or volunteer adult educator; irrespective of whether you are in one of the many programs of family literacy, workplace literacy, school-based ABE or literacy, or perhaps in one of the many types of English or French as a Second Language or language teaching with adults, based on the proven experience of others through pilot testing, this guide will help you become a better, more professional educator. And, since none of us is alone in this literacy work, it will help your program become stronger and more professional for the benefit of all involved, including the learners whom we serve.

THREE WAYS TO USE THIS GUIDE FOR STAFF DEVELOPMENT

1) In Urban Settings: An earlier version of this book was successfully pilot-tested through the Greater New Orleans Literacy Alliance for six weeks during the spring of 2005. The "trial-run experience" in Greater New Orleans gives an example of a way to use this guide in an urban setting, but it is not the only way to use this guide in an urban or a more densely populated area. The pilot included basic literacy, ABE, ESL, and GED teachers, as well as coordinators and administrators from six programs. All were in either community-based or publicly funded programs. Participants first read a chapter and kept learning journals, documenting their thoughts. This early step was assisted with the help of Blackboard—an electronic discussion program used across the programs involved. They then met at one of the program sites. Actually, they chose to rotate the meeting places to each of the program sites so the co-learners could come to know each other's programs better.

They met for chapter-end group meetings; these were facilitated by a team of two experienced facilitators, one female and one male. The male was the director of a local literacy provider agency; the female was an independent specialist in adult learning. The co-learners in their *learning circle*, as it will be called, decided which of the chapter-end activities to engage in and which of the suggested additional readings they wanted to take up and discuss further. Adult literacy student learners from the six provider agencies were also engaged as active members in some of the learning circle discussions.

Moving through this guidebook, the participants were able to assess changes in their own and others' perspectives using the journaling and dialogue processes. They also were able to effectively assess their newly acquired knowledge and skills in the learning circle, as well as back in their classrooms. They could also assess larger changes across their entire programs with the benefit of action research, as discussed in the last chapter of this guide.

At the time of this writing, it is anticipated that some will go on to join the current facilitators as mentors/facilitators for the next round(s) of professional development for other practitioners of other programs.

This model works well if people are in proximity and can meet regularly. It can also be conducted *within programs* without cross-program involvement. Nor does it need an electronic Blackboard communications program or an organizing facilitator, since this guide is written so it can be used by individuals and by groups, both in programs and across programs. But, as experience has taught me, there needs to be a commitment to read and engage regularly each week. Furthermore, the New Orleans pilot suggested the whole program takes about six weeks, but it all depends on how often the learning circle meets and communicates.

2) In Rural Settings: Sometimes in rural settings—even in urban settings, actually—it is not possible for practitioners to meet regularly on a face-to-face basis. In these cases, practitioners in programs can individually read the chapters, keep their journals, then discuss each chapter and the chapter-end questions with the activities and further readings without meeting with other programs on a regular basis, or at all. Of course, communicating and sharing by distance media using listservs, a platform like Blackboard, or audio technologies can help create a regionwide learning circle, but any group of two or more of teachers, tutors, and administrators in a rural program can simply work though the guide on their own.

Having met as a program-based learning circle by distance or in person, programs can take what they have discussed to a professional development gathering at an annual conference or an annual professional development meeting. This process could be orchestrated across programs during the year and organized in advance of the annual gathering by an administrator or facilitator. Therefore, professional development would not be a one- or two-day "expert-lead workshop at this year's annual conference." Instead, it would be a process of "experts collaborating" for several weeks or months in their regional programs, perhaps "cross-pollinating" across programs electronically along the way at strategic points—such as at chapter-endings—and the progress of each of the learning circles would be discussed and evaluated annually at the annual conference or meeting. Professional development should become a "frame of mind" rather than an "event." This guide can be of some help in this.

3) Self-Directed: But not everyone learns the same way. Not everyone wants to be part of a group. If by circumstances or choice you prefer to work through this guide by yourself, it just may be the best approach *for you.* Simply follow the chapters, the readings/further readings, and engage in the activities in your own work using the learning journal technique. But, I need to add, there is usually a direct benefit to sharing our thoughts, reflections, experiences, and successes with another. Through "inter-subjectivity" (Spiegelberg, 1960), we exchange views and can gain both a new sense of distance on our own activities and a way of seeing ourselves from a different perspective. No literacy practitioner is an island.

I suggest that you first consider the role your students might play—irrespective of the model adopted—and then try to think of someone whom you would be comfortable communicating with as you move through this guide. Perhaps you can find someone in literacy/ABE who will work through this guide simultaneously with you and communicate by e-mail, at least at chapter-end points. A "co-learner of one" may be all you need. In the final analysis, this program begins and ends with you, but it will be enriching if you make use of dialogue on the two levels I have described here.

ACKNOWLEDGMENTS

I would like to acknowledge the staff at the Literacy Alliance of Greater New Orleans, especially Peg Reese, Rachel Nicolosi, Adult Learning specialist Val Uccellani, and facilitator Doug Anderson who enthusiastically piloted an earlier version of this guide with literacy practitioners in New Orleans through the spring and early summer of 2005. I want to especially acknowledge those same practitioners who "took a risk" and participated in the pilot and, who heroically regrouped after Hurricane Katrina to finish the pilot. I also want to acknowledge my friend and colleague, Michael Cowan, for his unflagging support on this and other projects. I want to acknowledge Beth Bingman, who helped me with the survey on professionalism referred to in this guide book, and those many literacy practitioners who responded to the survey, including: Art La Chance, Dorothy Taylor, Sharon Flavin Cox, Norene Peterson, Patricia Theriault, Melissa Monti, Cynthia Fischer, Peggy Greenwald, Cindy Vermette, and my friend from Penn State days, Sue Snider. For the photographs and background materials on the Moonlight Schools, I want to acknowledge the generous help of Yvonne Baldwin. I also want to acknowledge the staff of the Hull House archival collection at the University of Illinois, Chicago, especially Pat Bakunis. The staff at the National Archives of Canada helped with the photos of Frontier College, and James Morrison—the Frontier College historian—was most generous and helpful with photos of Frontier College. My friend and colleague, Pierre Walter, gave valuable feedback on the Frontier College section, and Frontier College President, John O'Leary, was also highly supportive throughout. I also want to acknowledge Kathy MacKenzie at the St. Francis Xavier University Archives for her guidance and help with the photos of the Antigonish Movement. Ian Fleming with the YMCA archives in Toronto has also been extremely helpful. I want to acknowledge and thank those who read and responded to early drafts, including Patricia Cranton and Leona English. And thank you to Ron Cervero and Sharan Merriam, Series Editors, for their guidance, their amazing patience, and their faith in this project. Finally, thank you to Mary Roberts and Elaine Rudd at Krieger Publishing for believing in this book.

THE AUTHOR

Allan Quigley earned his bachelor of arts and his master of arts degrees at the University of Regina, Saskatchewan, Canada. He earned his doctorate in adult and continuing education at Northern Illinois University.

Following three years as a volunteer teacher in India with Canadian University Services Overseas, he began teaching adult literacy in 1972 in Northern Saskatchewan, Canada. He has since worked in Canadian community colleges—one of which he helped found in Regina, Saskatchewan—working as an adult literacy and basic education teacher, a programmer, an administrator, and a community developer. He was later the administrator for the GED, ESL and Adult Education programs with the government of Saskatchewan. After receiving his doctorate, he was Director of University Affairs Branch with the same government. He then spent ten years as a professor of adult education at Penn State University and joined St. Francis Xavier University in Nova Scotia, Canada, in 1997. He has researched and published extensively on the topic of adult literacy and his work is internationally known.

Besides teaching in the graduate program at St. Francis Xavier, he is currently a member of a mayor's literacy advisory committee helping with the rebuilding of New Orleans following Hurricane Katrina. He is also involved in the establishment of two new Knowledge Centers in Canada: the Adult Learning Knowledge Centre in New Brunswick and the Adult Health and Knowledge Centre in British Columbia. In addition, he is involved in researching the topic of authenticity in teaching in the literacy field, and is planning an edited book on the historical foundations of adult literacy and basic education in several industrialized nations.

INTRODUCTION

HERE'S WHAT YOU'LL NEED TO USE THIS GUIDE TO BEST EFFECT

1. **A journal.** This will usually be referred to in this guide as a "learning journal." It can be a notebook, a hardbound booklet, a diary, or space on your computer. You will be using it a lot through these chapters. A learning journal is a place to capture more than a description of events, more than your thoughts of the moment. A learning journal should also give you a consistent place to write down your questions, your criticisms, your reactions, and your on-going reflections on what you will be reading and discussing in this guide. And, it should also give you the space to discuss how you are feeling about the process itself. It will also give you a chance to look back at what you wrote a few days ago—or a few weeks ago. If you are anything like me, what seems clear and "memorable" right now, this very moment, won't be so memorable in a few days. Finally, a learning journal will be one of the keys we will be using to see changes in perspectives and daily practice. So, give journaling a try and remember to keep your learning journal up to date. This book will remind you to make your entries along the way.

2. **A group of co-learners and a learning circle.** Your co-learners should come from your program, be closely associated with your program, or be familiar with it. When they gather in a learning circle, you will be discussing your reflections from your journal and referring to the context of your program.

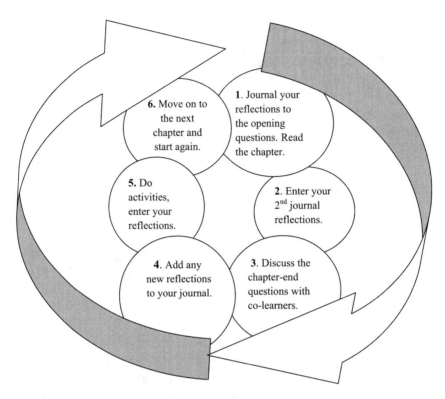

Figure 1 The six steps in the professional development process of this guide.

Besides those who are new to adult literacy and basic education, try to have the circle include "seasoned practitioners" who have more experience with the rewards, failures, and frustrations that come with adult literacy and basic education. Some will want students involved in all or some of the learning circle meetings as well.

3. **Access to a library**. This will become apparent as you go along, but each chapter offers you an (optional) Further Reading List so you can learn more about the issues raised. A good library with an inter-library lending service will be extremely helpful.

THE SIX-STEP PROCESS IN USING THE GUIDE

This dialogical guide will be most effective if it is *not* used in a passive way. It is designed to lead to activity and to change.

A CHECKLIST OF THE STEPS INVOLVED

1. First, think about the pre-chapter questions at the beginning of each chapter and write your thoughts in your learning journal. Only then, read through a chapter.

2. Reflect on what you have read in the chapter and then take a few minutes to write your thoughts a second time in your learning journal. Have they now changed in any way?

3. Now, discuss the pre- and post-entries with your co-learners. As noted already, a small group of four to seven can be very effective, but even one to three friends can make up a great learning circle. It should meet weekly if possible—especially at the outset of the dialogical process we are about to enter.

4. Revisit your journal with any further thoughts following the meeting of your co-learners.

5. Engage in one or more chapter-end learning activities with your co-learners, if at all possible, and make on-going journal entries while you work on an activity.

6. Then, repeat the cycle with the next chapter, and move on using the same cycle, chapter by chapter.

7. But one last point: After every chapter is finished, be sure to look back to see what you wrote, and summarize your reflections. Look for changes in where you began and how you modified or changed your thinking as you worked your way through the chapter. Consider what changed in your assumptions, if anything, and why changes have occurred, or not. You just might surprise yourself (and your co-learners too).

TWO QUESTIONS YOU MAY HAVE

Two very valid questions may arise as you start this program.

- **"Can I Really Make Any Changes in My Day-to-Day Practice?"**

You may have a "set" curriculum in your program, you may have very few resources to work with, or you may be surrounded by years of tradition and colleagues who simply say: "This is the way we have always done things around here." You may be in a program that, for the most part, not only works but works quite well. So, why enter this process?

Ask yourself this: "Is everyone satisfied in my program?" "Including me?" "Are all the learners entirely satisfied with the program?" Consider: "What is my dropout rate?" "My student attendance rate?" Ask: "Could I and others in my program be doing a better job?" And: "Could we not be doing a better job across the city, the region, the state, province, or territory?"

If my 40 years in adult literacy has taught me anything, it has taught me three things: *No two learners are alike.* We must continually work to find the best approach for the learners who come to our programs. Secondly, *there are many, many ways to teach.* Each has its benefits; there are very few "hard and fast rules" without exceptions. Finally, *professional development should not be considered a luxury or an "afterthought" or "that workshop being organized for next month."* Professional development is a necessary part of being an adult educator in today's changing, challenging world.

To the concern that "nothing can change or will change," I would say there is more flexibility in the teaching methods we can typically use and in the curricula we can develop and adapt in adult literacy than in virtually any other area of education— including prison literacy and GED preparation. However, if you find you indeed have no flexibility in your teaching methods, no flexibility in your curriculum, no room to alter how you administer your program, *then I would urge you to ask why this is.* In my view, it should be okay to take some risks, to try new ideas, and, yes, as we go forward, to fall occasionally—in the adult literacy field, there is always someone who will catch you.

Still, there's the hardest question of all:

- **"Where Do I Find the Time?"**

Time is always our enemy. But look at it this way: If you are interested in doing a better job for your students and yourself, if you have certain questions and issues that "itch" and you can't figure out how to deal with them, if you have a desire to enjoy your work and take more pride in what you do, isn't it better to try to address these problems head-on in an organized way with colleagues than to waste even more time struggling with them in isolation? How many times has the wheel been reinvented in literacy? We should be able to build, not reinvent. Moreover, why can't learning be fun for both students and teachers alike? We work at making learning as pleasant as possible for our learners, so why can't we, the educators, make our learning a stimulating experience that gives back energy and rewards us too?

Experience tells me that finding the time to do this professional development program comes by insisting on a few hours of our own. It should not be asking too much of our program, or family, or friends for an hour or two per week in the work schedule, or an hour or two in our personal lives simply to improve in what we do in literacy. Finding the time is finding the ways to organize the time. Others may need to give you a bit of space; ask for that space. You deserve it.

So, let's begin

CHAPTER 1

"The Higher We Climb": What Is a Professional?

Research that produces nothing but books will not suffice.
—Kurt Lewin

I once had a student who wrote me the following note at the bottom of one of her assignments: "I'm amazed at this program of Adult Education. It's like climbing a set of stairs. With every step I take, I can see farther." Her comment made my day. And my year.

I want to begin here because it seems to me that this is essentially how we would want all of our students to feel as they move through our programs. Don't we hope they will see a bigger world, and see it more clearly? Don't we work to try to have them gain more confidence as they progress, hoping they will feel greater satisfaction as they sense they are gaining confidence? Even if they aren't always "amazed" as they climb the stairs of our programs, given the types of negative, often painful experiences so many of our learners have experienced with past schooling, we wish that more will say learning is "not so bad after all." Or, "I never knew that learning can actually *be fun!*"

With these thoughts in mind, let's begin with a few opening questions for your journal. Your journal reflections on them will be the basis for the discussions you will have at chapter-end when you sit down with your co-learners.

OPENING QUESTIONS TO BEGIN YOUR LEARNING JOURNAL

Each time, enter today's date, and write any information you want as background, including your thoughts, concerns, anxieties, or hopes about this professional development program—and whatever else you want to begin with. Then take a few minutes to write down your responses and reflections on these questions:

1. What does it mean to act *unprofessionally*? How would you define this term?

2. What does it mean to act *professionally*? How would you define this?

3. Where does *professionalism* come from? That is, how does one learn to be professional?

4. What does it mean to act professionally *in your own program setting*? Do you see it quite often? What are some good examples of this?

5. Do you think most adult educators in other literacy or ABE programs—*those outside your own*—act in a professional manner? What are some examples of this?

6. What would you suggest needs to be done to make adult literacy and basic education a more professional field overall?

7. Would certification be the answer? Why? How would it work?

8. Do you have any other initial thoughts about professional development, professionalism, or professionalization? Please enter them in your journal.

Now, let's move on.

THE HEAD, THE HAND, AND THE HEART: A FRAMEWORK FOR PROFESSIONALISM

Professional development, as envisioned in this guide, should be like the staircase my student described. Like the stairs, this guide is about getting better at our practice but also about *knowing* we are getting better, and why. The climb we will take should take us beyond basic technical skills and essential knowledge, and provide what may well be some new perspectives on adults with low literacy skills. If successful, this guide will help you build and synthesize three elements: 1) *Knowledge*, 2) *Skills*, and 3) *Values*, moving you and your program toward a kind of "work wisdom." What the work-world calls "professionalism" will be referred to in this guide as the strengths of *the head, the hand, and the heart* (Lander, 1996). The knowledge that comprises professionalism may be thought of as the head. The skills can be thought of as the hand. And the heart can be thought of as the values we bring and need to continually reflect upon. This metaphor will be returned to repeatedly in this guide.

MY OWN VIEWS AND BIASES ON PROFESSIONALISM

I think it is only fair that I put my own thoughts (and biases) forward on how I see professionalism—and, of course, these are always changing for me too. This guide is a *guide* in the true sense of the word. It is not a cook book; it's more like a book on "how to cook." Why design this book in this way? My bias is that professionalism is a way of conducting oneself—especially in ambiguous and complex situations—not a series of "recipes on what to do." This way of conducting oneself includes a concern for being better at our work; it includes a concern for those who come to us looking for assistance and help; it includes seeking a higher level of competence in our skills and how well we make decisions; and it involves a concern for the larger field of practice. As I see it, to be critically reflective, to learn from our own learning, to truly draw from experience, to adapt and adopt the skills, techniques, and knowledge we experience and gain, to build a repertoire of "work wisdom" and the creative skills to realize and achieve our values—these are part of the lifelong process of professional development that can be achieved through a conscious journey. It is more than workshops or conferences or certificates. As Wlodkowski (1988) said of effective teaching, it is "not something one practices or performs, but something one enters and lives. It is a dimension" (p. 291).

In my view, becoming more professional is a dimension involving far more than having a framed certificate on the wall. Of course, I have no problem with certificates—I see them everywhere: in doctors' offices, teachers' offices, realtors' offices, barber shops and hair dressers' shops, automotive garages, to name a few. But ubiquitous as they are, I can't help but ask: "Why can't I get my car to run right?" And, "Why is it that so many people with certificates on the wall act so unprofessionally?" Who among us doesn't know about misdiagnoses and disastrous errors in the medical profession? The term "iatrogenisis" has been applied to what is known as "doctor-created disease" (Cervero, 1988, p. 27). Certificates, workshops, and courses can play a very important role in professional development, no question about it, but they certainly do not *guarantee* competence, knowledge, professionalism, or values, or even a level of professional civility for that matter (Queeney & English, 1994).

It is important to note that 14 U.S. states now either recommend or require adult literacy and basic education practitioners to have an adult education certificate before they can teach or administer adult literacy (Sabatini, Ginsberg & Russell, 2002; Sork & Welock, 1992), and the discussion is heating up on certification in Canada as well. Not surprisingly, some of these states don't actually enforce these requirements (Gilley & Galbraith, 1992). In fact, without a much greater investment in professional development, many states can't possibly fulfill these requirements. But the real question is if certification is the single answer to the professionalism issue (Koloski, 1989; Mattran, 1989). Before entering that thorny debate, wouldn't it be helpful to first ask, "What is a professional?" Let's look at the roots of this concept.

WHERE DOES THE CONCEPT OF "PROFESSIONALISM" COME FROM?

Unfortunately, many discussions on professionalism in our field begin with the deficit perspective. The view that literacy practitioners are in a state of deficit around skills and knowledge is quite pervasive in the literature. Interestingly, the values of literacy teachers, tutors, and administrators are usually not mentioned. And it is here that we are especially strong. Instead of beginning with perceived deficits, let's begin where we might want to begin with our own students. Where we are indisputably strong: with our own values.

According to the *Shorter Oxford English Dictionary*, as early as 1560 to "profess" meant to "affirm one's faith in or allegiance to (a religion, principle; God, a saint, etc.)" (Little, et al. 1970, p. 1593). The concept of a "profession" in the Middle Ages, therefore, was "the act or fact of professing . . . the declaration, promise, or vow made on entering a religious order . . . the fact of being professed in a religious order" (p. 1593). Isn't it interesting that the earliest definition was not about competence, or knowledge, or working full-time, or career aspirations, or having a framed diploma on the wall? It was about professing one's personal commitment to a vocation—to a calling.

Michael Collins, who has written extensively on this point in adult education, forcefully argues that professionalism, understood in its original and appropriate form, should be "unencumbered with a high concern for exclusive self-interests . . . [and] is very much in line with the practice of a vocation" (1991, p. 87). To "profess" is to be committed to something other than one's personal ambitions. Therefore, the largely absent topic of values should be re-introduced to our discussions in this whole area. As seen in the next sections, values are alive and well in adult literacy and basic education, even if they are greatly under-valued.

"THE BEST OF REASONS": BEGINNING WITH STRENGTH

In my experience, most in this field are closer to the original meaning of "profession" in their values than in any other area of education that I know of. After all, adult literacy teachers, tutors, and many administrators work part-time, or volunteer their time and energy to their program with little or no salary. They often have very few aspirations toward "career advancement" on the "ladder of literacy careerism"—there aren't many rungs to aspire to, in fact. The very concept of "careerism" in adult literacy is foreign, if not laughable. It is true that some gain social recognition in their family or community, but there are many easier ways to spend and volunteer one's time to gain far more social recognition and prestige. Most in our field are "givers" who believe that a little thing called "the printed and spoken word" matters. They know that enhanced reading, writing, and numeracy skills can make a difference—a dramatic, profound, transformative difference—to people's lives. To the lives of families. To whole communities. They know this vocation matters. In the many years I have been in adult literacy, I have mainly seen practitioners who are involved for what can only be called the best of reasons.

One of the greatest strengths of adult literacy practitioners is that most—obviously not all—practitioners in this field have faith that individuals can learn and change. Ours is a field that gives hope, and we receive hope back from learners. Ours is a field created and sustained out of compassion for others—and we gain compassion back. Ours is extremely strong in its values and, in this sense, is remarkably close to the original meaning and very essence of what it means to be "professional."

But are strong values enough? Faith, hope, and compassion are elements found in the early meaning of "professing" a commitment to a vocation, but they may not be the answer when decisions need to be made on topics like accountability, or quality assessment, or teaching learners with learning disabilities, or funding formulae. Skills and knowledge matter in this field (Merrifield, 1998). And this will be covered in this guide. But we must keep in mind the values and qualities that help define who we are.

Many other professions can only dream of having thousands of volunteers and part-time staff with the compassion and willingness to help others year after year. We need to begin our exploration of professionalism in this context, I think. We need to begin with *what we have, and should be proud of.* But this is not necessarily the view of everyone who researches and writes in our field. Since the debate on professionalism potentially affects us all, let's briefly look at the discussions in the literature.

A LOOK AT WHAT LITERACY PRACTITIONERS SAY

Through the decades—in fact through the centuries, as will be seen in the next chapter—the field of adult literacy and basic education has never lacked advice on what it should be doing differently. The most recent wave of advice comes in the context of today's literacy professionalism debate in America, a debate that is also gaining interest in Canada. Some, such as Susan Foster (1990), insist the field must "develop standards of practice that will guide instructors in what to teach, how to teach, how to be responsive to goals, needs and culture of the learner, and how to improve accountability" (pp. 79–80). For Foster, our field is tragically isolated from the K-12 schooling system, claiming: "Literacy programs are a bastard of the educational system—isolated from the mainstream and deprived of adequate resources for health, growth, and development" (p. 81). Others, such as Sabatini, Ginsberg, and Russell, also believe that "adult basic education has long been in the shadow of the K-12 education system" (2002, p. 206). They argue adult literacy and basic education could learn much from the experi-

ences of the schooling system for purposes of professionalization. In most cases, the advice offered is around ways to develop
enhanced skills and knowledge through formal studies (Smith
& Hofer, 2002).

In an opinion survey of 22 literacy practitioners across 14
states that I recently completed with a colleague, literacy practitioners with an average of 15 years of literacy experience
(ranging from 30 years to 3 years) said in response to the question: "What does it mean to be a 'professional'?" that, to be a
professional in the sense typically understood in most professions requires formal training and ongoing participation in continuing education. As one participant put it: "A professional [in
the broadest sense] is someone who is formally trained in the
area in which they are working, preferably with a degree and/or
certificate in that area." What was very interesting was that
there was typically a separation between what being a professional meant *in general terms* and what it should mean in the
field of adult literacy and basic education. As one participant
put it: "Unfortunately, it appears that simply having a college
degree makes one a 'professional.'"

When the questions turned specifically to adult literacy,
the consistent theme was that a mandatory certificate does not
guarantee professional conduct. This was pointed out repeatedly. While only 7 of the 22 believed certification of some kind
should be an essential component to achieve for professionalism
in adult literacy and basic education, the rest were highly skeptical of the value of certification. As a friend of mine put it: "One
does not fatten the pig by weighing it." There was a concern
that certification might actually have a negative impact on the
field. One said: "Bottom line—can a certification process identify, value, and validate qualities, skills, attributes that genu-
inely make a difference to adult learning?"

There were differing views of what professionalism should
mean in the literacy field. One participant put it succinctly:
"To act 'professionally' in literacy and adult education is to self-
educate in professional development, whether compensated or
not, to give one's highest level of expertise whether or not remu-

neration is commensurate with hours spent of intellectual investment." On the same theme, another participant replied that literacy practitioners act professionally when they view "students as most valued clients and attempt to engage their individual needs and goals within a high-quality program of basic skills instruction." Many felt practitioners were acting professionally in their daily conduct, even if this is rarely recognized or acknowledged outside the practice setting. According to one participant, if you want to see a professional, you usually don't have to look very far: "[Just look at] the people on the front lines who are dealing with . . . [learners'] reality every day, all day long. [Just go there] and you will see professionalism." This respondent added: "The very best adult literacy providers basically ignore the suggestions for standardized curriculum development and apply what works."

The theme of caring was one of the strongest point made. As one put it:

> This is by far the most dedicated group of people I have ever worked with. They are more dedicated to helping the misfortunate than the medical community, for instance. We don't charge money for services, we maintain a positive support at every opportunity, we cry with them, laugh with them, and see them through the best and the worst. We are truly like family.

These themes were continually repeated. Another put it this way: "To act professionally in adult literacy one is service-oriented, friendly and accountable. A professional is ethical and posses strong values, especially those pertaining to literacy and the population one serves." And the respondent then added: "I encounter this most of the time wherever I go in adult literacy."

Acting Professionally but Viewed as Non-Professionals

When questions turned to the image of the field, the participants were asked: "Do you think the field of adult literacy and basic education is now a profession?" The responses indicated a consistent sense of frustration and anger. One participant said that despite the fact that "our academic disciplines are strong" and our "adult education research is growing and ongoing, and advocacy is increasing," the field is not regarded as being professional or a profession. The lack of respect from outside—sometimes inside—the field was echoed over and over.

Nevertheless, as one participant put it, "We should work toward the goal of 'being' professional, and 'act professionally' . . . since neither we nor our programs are likely to be so recognized anytime soon." Reasons given for the perceived lack of respect included the long legacy of volunteerism and part-time employment. The severe lack of funding and lack of job security was cited time and again. One noted that, in the working conditions, there is "so little access to ongoing professional development (read, time to think, resources, information, access to print/internet/other colleagues/mentors)." Another argued our field is not "held in high regard, because our students are not respected."

For these and other reasons, the net result was, as one put it, "most of the practitioners act as professionals, but they get discouraged when they are part-time and treated as second-class citizens in their organizations." And sadly, many, many excellent teachers, tutors, and administrators have left the field while saying they loved the work. They did not want to leave but couldn't afford to stay.

I am not alone in hoping that enhanced professionalism and building greater pride in what we do will lead to a more positive impact on the future of this field (Beder, 1994). As I see it, it is the practitioners who carry our future in the final analysis—not academics, not politicians, not consultants. And practitioners are now raising their voices more and more for a truly stable, better recognized, and more respected field (Quigley, 2001; Quigley & Watkins, 2001). It is my fervent hope that this book will give the field an even more solid platform to stand on as we make the case for a better future for literacy. After all, if we don't do it, who will?

To Act Professionally Is to Bring Three Essential Qualities to Adult Literacy

In our survey, the general concept of professionalism was not always seen to be the same for adult basic education and literacy as for other professions. What seemed to separate the two constructs in the two types of contexts was values. On one hand, what should go into professional conduct in teaching and administering adult literacy was quite consistent. Education and training to build *knowledge* of the subjects and practice, and education or training to build the *skills* necessary for the job, were the first two required elements. But the third element was stressed repeatedly. In adult literacy, a professional needs to be a caring, compassionate, dedicated educator. One is held to a high standard on values in our field.

The first two qualities, education and training, did not of necessity have to come through certification or external standards. They could, for instance, be self-taught, learned in context with mentoring, and could be developed through continuing education. But values were not as easily taught, and it was simply agreed this should come with the teacher. Most pointed to this special quality in those whom they worked with.

In a study concerning the viability and desirability of having a code of ethics across mainstream adult education involving 249 adult educators in the U.S., as conducted by McDonald and Wood (1993), the voice of the adult basic educators came through loud and clear. As the researchers concluded, there are "already enough rules and regulations regarding their practice" (p. 253). And when it came to an imposed code of ethics for the wider field, as one adult basic educator said: "No code of ethics written could ever be as high as the code of ethics that I have set for myself as a person and an educator" (p. 249).

What is professionalism in adult literacy and basic education? As seen in Figure 1.1, it appears to be the combination of knowledge and skills, as required in any profession, but it also needs to involve caring, empathy, compassion, ethical conduct, and dedication to the learners' needs. I believe all three can be

KNOWLEDGE

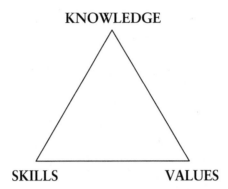

SKILLS   VALUES

Figure 1.1 Components in the Professionalism Construct

developed and enhanced in literacy practice, both alone and in groups, and this guide is designed to foster such development. Certification, as noted earlier, can also help, but it can easily lead to many frustrations at many levels, especially if it is naively assumed that models from other professions should be transplanted and imposed, ignoring the values, traditions, culture, traditions, and history that we have built over the course of two centuries, as will be seen in chapter two.

LOOKING AT WHAT THE LITERATURE TELLS US

Most of the literature on this topic in the mainstream field of adult education over the past several decades assumes the same three interconnected components comprise professionalism: 1) knowledge, 2) skills, and 3) values. These three are seen in Figure 1.1.

However, the three are rarely in balance in most discussions of professionalism, and the arguments that have arisen over professionalism in adult education and literacy are no exception. One of the three typically dominates the others in the triangle. Let's review the salient arguments on this in recent years.

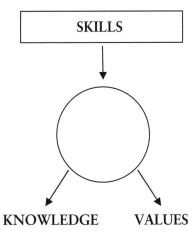

Figure 1.2 The Functionalist View: Professional Components with Skills and Competencies Most Significant

Professionalism: The Functionalist Approach

The longest standing and most widely known approach to professionalism is what Cervero (1988) has termed "the static approach" (p. 5; and see Houle, 1980). It takes a *functionalist viewpoint* of the issues (see Cervero, 1988). From this point of view, skills matter most in the functioning of any profession (Figure 1.2).

As early as 1910, Abraham Flexner (1910, 1915), one of America's dominant figures in the formation of schools and the systems they would operate, said one sets about measuring whether an occupation is a profession by looking first at *how well things function*. Effective functioning was everything for Flexner. To be considered a profession, an occupation must: (1) involve intellectual operations, (2) derive material from science, (3) involve definite and practical ends, (4) possess an educational communicable technique, (5) tend to self-organization, and (6) be altruistic.

This may sound straightforward, but as time went by the list of requirements for a profession ran to ridiculous lengths. As Cervero has said: "The major problem with this approach is the persistent lack of consensus about the criteria that should be used to define professions" (1988, p. 6). This is exactly what happened to adult education during the Adult Performance Level (APL) movement of the 1970s. At that time, teaching "measurable competencies" was to be the basis for all adult literacy curricula and testing (Mocker, 1974; Smith, 1978). However, since the functionalist approach could not move ahead without consensus on the criteria, the drive for competencies ran into problems. Inability to implement much of the curriculum followed. Later, Griffith and Cervero (1977) took a closer look at the APA tests that the U.S. Department of Education were requiring for adult basic education and for passing grades in the APL programs being adopted by many states. The two researchers found multiple examples of cultural bias. The skills and specific knowledge the test developers were considering "necessary" to function effectively in society were clearly based on white, middle-class values.

What about teacher competencies? As a mirror-image of the APL for students, the lists of competencies for alleged "effective teaching" in adult literacy education was growing longer and longer, and more contradictory. For instance, Mocker found and ranked no fewer than 291 competencies that he concluded were required for teachers of adult basic education to be "competent" (Mocker, 1974). Ironically, this "definitive" listing of skills so essential to be effective is now long forgotten.

Adult literacy and basic education was but one in the broad debate over competencies across education and training. As the lists grew and became more complicated, by the mid-1970s researchers were beginning to agree that the skills "required" by both students and ABE teachers alike were too arbitrary, and the theoretical framework for competencies was just too simplistic. The competencies didn't fit the realities of adult literacy education. Even though the term "functional literacy" was highly popular in the 1970s and 1980s (Collins, 1987; Quigley, 1987), the quest for learner competencies and the nationwide Adult Performance Level movement simply collapsed by the end of the 1980s taking the lists of teacher competencies with them. If this bandwagon left values out of the teacher equation, it also ignored the complexities of learner motivation. In fact, the entire affective domain was absent for both learner and teacher (Quigley, 1987). This competency-based approach has since come under criticism for being too mechanistic, too reductionist, too unworkable (Collins, 1983).

Nevertheless, many today favor the tradition of the functionalist approach to adult literacy and argue that skills and competencies for students need to be at the forefront. There are many calls for some type of standardized curricula across ABE, some pointing to the K-12 school system as the best model. For example, Chisman (1990) argued it is unfortunate that there are no "commonly accepted criteria for how [ABE] teachers should be trained or how curricula should be structured" (p. 18). As seen earlier, Foster has argued that "We need to develop standards of practice that will guide our instructors in what to teach, how to teach, how to be responsive to goals, needs and the culture of the learner, and how to improve accountability" (pp. 79–80). Others have explored the value of skills-based certification for practitioners (Sabatini, Ginsburg, & Russell, 2002), and the same arguments appear around discussions on accountability in literacy education.

On the other side of the argument, Belzer and St. Clair (2003) recently reviewed the recent adult literacy literature and found many "demands for a professional development that [are] closely related to an agreed-upon body of knowledge and set of skills that are distinctive to adult education and demonstrate competence" (p. 17). However, they hasten to argue that such "systems may be more effective *if they are flexible enough to reflect the diversity of the work force and provide a variety of alternatives for acquiring and demonstrating expertise* [italics added]" (p. 18).

History has taught us that flexibility is hard to achieve in the functionalist approach. It has been practically impossible to decide on the "ultimate list required." Even if a consensus can be reached, requirements change, then change again, in the complex work of human behavior. Scholars such as James (1989, 1992) argued against a skills-approach to curricula in the context of an argument against skills-based certification, saying:

"Certification [across adult education] is not only impractical but also unattainable for the entire field and, therefore, should not be implemented on a large-scale basis" (1992, p. 130). As James (1989) put it when looking at the broad field of adult education: "Certification alone will not legitimate the field; only striving for excellence within adult education can do that" (p. 95; and see Belzer, 2005).

Professionalism: The Conflict Approach

The debate in the literature over the past decade shows that many mainstream adult education scholars are arguing that we must return to the moral base and principles of the 19th- and early 20th-century vision of adult education (Quigley, 1989). The rising tide in the mainstream literature is not about more technical skills or authorized knowledge acquisition for professionalism. Mainstream adult education is rediscovering its roots in the form of *personal responsibility*. Whereas "altruism" appeared last in Flexner's early list of requirements for a profession, as seen earlier, it is much farther up the ladder of desirable qualities now. In the past decade, Cervero and Wilson (1994, 2001), among others (Caffarella, 1994; Merriam, 1991), have introduced terms such as "responsible planning," "ethical decision-making," and "morals" into the vocabulary—such terms were rarely seen in the literature even a decade ago.

In fact, there is rising interest across mainstream adult education in spirituality (English & Gillen, 2001), which all goes to the question of *why* we practice adult education in the first place. Brookfield, one of America's most prolific authors, has written on topics such as "moral learning" (1998). With a view we would not have seen a decade ago, Merriam has argued that "programs of graduate study [in adult education] should present research as a value-laden, moral activity" (1991, pp. 60–61). The day when mainstream adult education literature, research, and practice were primarily concerned with questions of "how," "what," and "when" has shifted across the continuum to the "why" of doing what we do.

This move toward a *more responsible, not only more responsive*, field of practice has brought with it higher expectations on clarity of personal purpose, higher expectations concerning critical reflection on practice, and increased interest in the ways teachers and practitioners can learn about their own work and make their own decisions based on ethics and self-direction.

On professionalism, the larger field of mainstream adult education and training has effectively moved past asking others for external rules, or codes, or mandates, or certification regulations. Broadly speaking, mainstream adult education and training are advocating that practitioners work out of a concern for responsible practice and critical self-reflection deriving from culturally-recognized ethics and values. In program planning and in areas of adult education professional practice, it is now values that matter, and come first, as depicted in Figure 1.3.

This shift in our understanding of professionalism and practice has, in part, occurred because of the introduction of the "Conflict Viewpoint" (Cervero, 1988, p. 26) in the professionalism discourse.

Behind the struggle over criteria seen in the functionalist viewpoint—a struggle which could mean the difference between hundreds of practitioners having the certification to work and earn a living, or not—lies issues of power. The conflict viewpoint says there really is very little difference between an occupation and a profession, because those declaring themselves professionals "have secured a monopoly for their services in the market-place" (p. 26). In this view, professions have built up an "aura of mystery about professional work and [promoted] myths about . . . the relative difficulty [of their work]" (p. 26; Haug, 1975). McKnight put it this way. The conflict viewpoint says professions are telling us: "We are the solution to your problems; you don't know what the problem is; you can't understand the problem or the solution" (1977, p. 116). Illich made it even clearer that simply having "the power to prescribe" (1977, p. 17) has come to mean the power to be a profession.

The conflict viewpoint seeks to debunk the mystique built around professions and reveals how the structures they are part

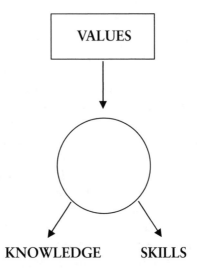

Figure 1.3 The Conflict View: Professional Components With Values as Most Significant

of are really about hierarchies, inaccessibility, and the power to control others' lives. In this view, far from altruism, vocation or a "calling," many professions are so powerful and self-contained they are largely unwilling to enter self-critique or radical self-assessment from the inside out.

The job of today's professional, says those in the conflict school of thought, is to be far more critical of professions as currently structured, return to earlier values, place values at the heart of professional conduct, and seriously question the social-structural levels of many professional organizations in order to return to more self-responsibility both at the individual and systemic levels.

CAN'T WE TAKE A MORE BALANCED APPROACH?

Reading this, you may wonder, "Must it be an all-or-nothing proposition when we turn to our field of adult literacy and basic education?" In our field, can we not draw from the best of both of these worlds? Because we are not (yet) locked into the functionalist approach and are not (yet) in a state of conflict through the conflict approach, we have a chance to shape this field of ours. I want to suggest we can build knowledge and skills *without* leaving out or sacrificing the deep values so many hold. We can work toward more balance than seen so far as our way forward.

It may be hard to think of professionalism in any terms other than the traditional static ones seen earlier in the functionalist approach. It may also be hard to think of professionalism from the conflict viewpoint, where values dominate and responsible practice is the touchstone of professionalism. But it is not hard to see that perhaps there are questions that arise for adult literacy concerning *both* positions.

Furthermore, absent from any of the arguments seen thus far, we could well ask: "Why has the adult learner no voice, no role in professionalism when it is ultimately the learners' lives we are all talking about?" After all, "Are we not supposed to be serving learner needs in our search for professionalism? Is this only about practitioners' needs?"

The over-arching question here is: "Can we not explore approaches to professionalism that bring the best qualities of the functionalist viewpoint and the conflict viewpoint together with a true openness *to the real needs of learners*?" Can we not find a way to balance the three components of the skills-values-knowledge framework based on what the learner wants and needs? Teachers and tutors can help adult learners see options; we can help learners gain skills, knowledge, and values clarification. Why can't we do this for ourselves? How? We can do so by becoming better informed, more skilled, and more critically reflective of our own work, ourselves, and our field, through a balanced approach to professional development, as seen next.

Professionalism: Toward a Praxis Learning Model

Building on the work of the authors we have seen thus far, and the two perspectives on professionalism discussed, let us suggest that "seeing farther" and becoming more professional can occur by focusing on: 1) skills, 2) knowledge, and 3) our values. A three-part, balanced approach.

This is not a unique idea. Donald Schön (1983) asked how the world's top physicians, architects, musicians, and athletes learn. After all, they are at the peak of their professions and there are really no teachers left for them. Schön found it was neither techniques nor methods alone that make the world's top professionals and keep them there. He found they have an exceptional talent for learning from experience, for reflecting on what they have learned, for learning from others, and for synthesizing learning into their current knowledge and skills base. They apply critical reflection in a very sophisticated way.

Schön puts great faith in critical reflection. This can be seen as the praxis approach and is suggested as a way forward for professionalism and professional development in the field of adult literacy.

LEARNING FROM PRAXIS

Praxis, according to the *International Dictionary of Adult and Continuing Education* (1990) is "a term . . . Freire has adapted to refer to the congruence between individual reflection and the action that results from it" (Jarvis, 1990, p. 272). This means the action and change for professional development comes not from external standards requirements, or requirements for licensure, or from external rewards or "punishments." Rather, professional development through "praxis" here means *personal* reflection and the action arising from it. Personal initiative for learning is the approach being suggested in this guide, but it is done so with the suggestion that inter-dependence is a most effective approach for us and our learners.

Here is a process of making meaning of events with others and being better able to learn from and with them in order to deal with the new situations we encounter. The onus is on the self, but we look to others in our field who are working on simi-

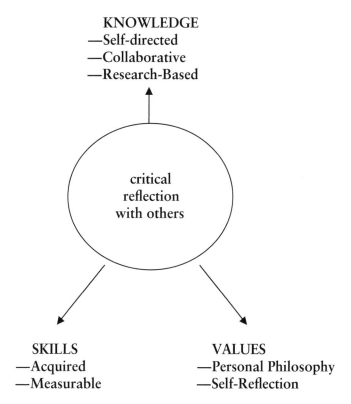

KNOWLEDGE
—Self-directed
—Collaborative
—Research-Based

critical
reflection
with others

SKILLS
—Acquired
—Measurable

VALUES
—Personal Philosophy
—Self-Reflection

Figure 1.4 A Praxis Approach to Professional Components in Balance

lar ground for advice and support. This leads us to a praxis-based figure like the one seen in Figure 1.4. From this praxis viewpoint, professionalism derives from within; it is merely developed from without. It can be observed, it can be experienced and, in many ways, it can be measured.

PUTTING THE PRAXIS-APPROACH INTO PRACTICE

This guide is intended to help practitioners develop as professionals. Discussion questions, professional development activities, and follow-up readings appear at the end of each chapter; each chapter is written to help enhance skills, knowledge, and values. But how can anyone know she or he is changing as a result of this guide? There needs to be a way of reflecting on what is happening and seeing that reflection for yourself. As earlier discussed, a learning journal will capture your thoughts, your reflections, your opinions, your doubts and your successes—and you can look back at your journal to evaluate your own change and see what changes have occurred at the chapter-end (and see English & Gillen, 2001).

MOVING ON WITH JOURNALLING

Having your initial thoughts down in your journal from the opening of this chapter, it is now time to go back to your journal and add any new thoughts you have since we are about at the end of this chapter. Please enter your second set of reactions, thoughts, questions, and any other notes you want to make. Then please go through the Suggested Questions for Discussion that follow and make entries. Then discuss the chapter-end questions and your recorded reflections with your co-learners. Make any new entries following the meetings of your learning circle. If you can, try some or all of the Suggested Activities. Remember, we "learn by doing" in this guide, so go to the Suggested Reading List for further information on the topics mentioned.

But please remember before going on to Chapter 2 to look back in your learning journal to see what you thought *at the opening of the chapter* concerning the initial questions. Ask what the reflections were of others in your circle. As you go, ask if each chapter is making an impact on your values, knowledge, and skill levels. If so, how and why? If not, why not?

CHECKING FOR PROGRESS

The evaluation of progress does not have to stop here. Other measures can also be used to see if the skills, knowledge, and values changes are making a difference in your practice and program. It may be too soon to look for major change, but you can begin asking: What is the learner retention rate in my classroom? What is the staff retention rate? What are the learner satisfaction and staff satisfaction levels? As we get to the next chapters, you can well begin to ask: Is camaraderie improving in my program? Are learner progress rates and outcomes improving? Do I see evidence that learner performance is improving both during and following my program? What about any structural or procedural improvements in administrative processes? Are they changing?

CHAPTER 1 DISCUSSION TOPICS FOR CONSIDERATION IN YOUR LEARNING JOURNAL AND LEARNING CIRCLE

- What do you and your co-learners think it means to be a "professional" in general; that is, in any work setting? Put another way, how would you define this word?
- What does it mean to be a "professional" in literacy and adult basic education? Is there any difference between literacy and other work settings?
- What does it mean to "act professionally" in your own program setting? Do you see it quite often? What are some examples of this?
- Does "professionalism" come from having certain knowledge, or certain attitudes and values, or is it a result of a person's skills? If it is all three, which matters most?
- Having thought about your own program and components of professionalism, are there ways to enhance the level of professionalism across your own program?
    Who should take the lead on this?
    Over what period of time should this occur?
    Can you form an action plan?
- What would you suggest needs to be done to make adult literacy and basic education a more professional field overall?

CHAPTER 1
ACTIVITY OPTIONS FOR FOLLOW-UP

Try undertaking one or more of the following suggested activities alone, with your students, or with your co-learners. Or create other activities that might help explore the concept and practical aspects of professionalism.

1) Possibly with the help of your students, conduct an interview survey or questionnaire survey asking: "What do you think professionalism means?" in any setting *other than your own program*. Ask, "What does professional conduct mean?" Ask, "What does it mean to act 'unprofessionally'?" "How does one improve one's professionalism?" It could be conducted in a doctor's office, or a dentist's office, or a grocery store, or a school, or in any combination of these, and others.

2) Ask questions similar to those you just asked in your *own* program and see how they compare. What have others in your learning circle found concerning the nature of professionalism? Are the results different or the same?

3) Conduct a survey of your own students' views, or have them survey other students in your program. Compare their answers to what you and your colleagues said in your learning circle. What, in other words, do your learners think and expect?

4) With your co-learners or learning circle, consider the "most unprofessional action I have ever seen." Go through the events and consider what went into this event. Why do you think it happened? What could have prevented it?

5) Read one of more of the readings in the following list. Discuss them in your learning circle.

CHAPTER 1: FURTHER READING

On Journal Writing

English, L., & Gillen, M. (2001). *Promoting journal writing in adult education*. New Directions for Adult and Continuing Education, No. 90. San Francisco: Jossey-Bass.

On Critical Reflection

Brookfield, S. (1990). Using critical incidents to explore learners' assumptions. In J. Mezirow & Assoc. (Eds.), *Fostering critical reflection in adulthood*, (pp. 177–193). San Francisco: Jossey-Bass.

Schön, D. A. (1983). *The reflective practitioner*. New York: Basic Books.

On Professionalism and Professional Development

Belzer, A., & St. Clair, R. (2003). *Opportunities and limits: An update on adult literacy education. Columbus, OH: The Ohio State University (ERIC information Series No. 391)*.

Sabatini, J. P., Ginsburg, L., & Russell, M. (2002). Professionalization and certification for teachers in adult basic education. In J. Comings, B. Garner, & C. Smith (Eds.), *Annual review of adult learning and literacy*, Vol. 3, pp. 203–247.

Cervero, R. (1988). *Effective continuing education for professionals*. San Francisco: Jossey-Bass.

Collins, M. (1991). *Adult education as vocation*. New York: Routledge.

Smith, C., & Hofer, J. (2002). Pathways to change: A summary of the findings from NCSALL's staff development study. *Focus on Basics, 5* (D), 1, 3–7.

On Controversies Over Professionalization and Practice

Cervero, R., Wilson, A., & Associates (Eds.). (2001). *Power in practice: Adult education and the struggle for knowledge and power in society.* San Francisco: Jossey-Bass.

James, W. B. (1992). Professional certification is not needed in adult and continuing education. In M. Galbraith & B. Sisco (Eds.), *Confronting controversies in challenging times: A call for action* (pp. 125–131). New Directions for Adult and Continuing Education, No. 54. San Francisco: Jossey-Bass.

Rosenkranz Cameron, C. (1989). Certification should be established. In B. W. Krietlow & Assoc. (Eds.), *Examining controversies in adult education*, pp. 84–96. San Francisco: Jossey-Bass.

CHAPTER 2

Building On Our Past For A More Professional Future

A profession that does not know where it has been is unlikely to know where it is going.

—Edwin Smith

As was discussed in the first chapter, we have a deep tradition of caring and giving in this field. But, we typically have had no way to reflect on or draw inspiration from our rich history. Part of the reason for this—and there are many reasons—is that we live almost exclusively in the "practice moment" in adult literacy education. The field's orientation is toward the present moment, and we worry about the future when time permits. Moreover, there is a public if not political view that illiteracy and low literacy should have been "fixed" by now. The public has had endless campaigns and political promises through time (Arnove & Graff, 1987). Why research or celebrate a "failed past?" But is this kind of assumption based on facts?

Even if we aren't particularly aware of it, we have a proud past waiting to be reclaimed. Little wonder we have trouble even beginning to think of adult literacy and basic education as a profession if we have so little memory; so little to draw inspiration from. Florence Nightingale is known in nursing, John Dewey in education, and military, sports and music "legends" are well known and celebrated. Who are our heroes and heroines? Let's return to our learning journals to think about the following questions.

CHAPTER 2: PRE-CHAPTER QUESTIONS FOR YOUR LEARNING JOURNAL

Turning now to this second chapter, please enter the date and any information you want as background to this chapter in your journal. Please take a few minutes to reflect on and write down your reflections on these questions:

1. If you were asked to name two or three major figures in adult literacy education through history—two or three heroines or heroes of literacy—who would they be?

2. When did your *own program* begin? Who founded it? Why did she/he/they do so?

3. Why do you think organizations, states, and countries begin teaching adults to read in organized programs in the first place? What were some of the reasons for their choosing to fund and sponsor adult literacy programs?

4. Why do you think our history of literacy is typically so undervalued? Why is it so absent from the literacy literature, from literacy conferences, from policy decisions?

5. Do you think the history of literacy should play a more significant role in our field? In your daily practice? If "yes," then how? If "no," why not?

6. Enter any other thoughts, questions, or concerns you might have about literacy and history in your learning journal.

Robert Carlson has stated that historical research is the most effective method for understanding practice that we have available to us because "it provides the sort of perspective that lets us determine where we have come from, what we are doing and why, where we appear to be going, and how we might influence events in a humane direction" (cited in Merriam & Simpson, 2000, p. 94). Unfortunately, we have virtually no historical research on adult literacy and basic education; therefore, we tend to lack this perspective. We have only a few history chapters in mainstream adult education books, a handful of articles on particular historical events and movements in adult literacy, two or three out-of-print books, and a few books in Britain that claim to be about adult literacy but are really about mainstream adult education by any North American definition. Moreover, it is rare for local programs to publish their own history, present them at conferences, or discuss them with funding agencies, students, or the media. This seems odd when we are so committed to trying to honor and build pride in learners' cultures and history. It is also odd in that so many feel a strong sense of allegiance for their program. Policy makers rarely seek to fund much more than immediate program delivery, or evaluations of programs, so it is understandable that we have so little history research and such difficulty learning from our successes and failures through time.

Yet when I speak to audiences of literacy practitioners and talk about some of the literacy landmarks I've been learning about in England, the United States, Canada, New Zealand, and Australia, most are absolutely fascinated. It seems to me that many practitioners in state after state, province after province, city after city know their local practitioners and programs very well, know their state and local adult education officials quite well if they are publicly funded, and typically work hard at learning about the latest trends in program grants or funding, but beyond the "here-and-now-and-next-year's-budget," it is uncommon to meet anyone who can talk about how their program's mission has evolved through time, or what lessons are to be learned from programs that have survived and flourished for decades. Some, like Frontier College in Canada, have survived for over a century. Others have disappeared. Why?

Let's take a closer look at this as a systemic issue for professionalism before turning to some of the stories of our past.

THE CHALLENGES OF PROFESSIONALIZING

How does one build pride in a field of practice? The absence of a sense of past brings a sense of impermanence. A sense in our case that adult literacy education is a temporary "movement." There is a kind of hegemony in society, even in our own field, that says we are a collection of programs and volunteers that will not be needed when the literacy problems are all "fixed." Any review of the policies over the 20th century will show that campaigns for literacy have promised over and over that illiteracy will be eradicated within three years, five years, by the turn of the century, and so on and so on (Quigley, 1987). But the goals are never attained. Where did we get the notion that illiteracy will one day be "eliminated" in America or Canada anyway? It certainly did not come by looking back at our centuries-old history of adult literacy education that clearly says that neither the United States nor Canada has ever been fully literate (Arnove & Graff, 1987). Rather, here's what Edwin Smith concluded after looking back over the history of literacy events in the United States:

> Over the years, in times of crisis, the main body of Americans kept rediscovering the literacy problems and, over the years, hastily contrived solutions to the problem were invented or re-invented. As the crisis passed, so did the concern of America's leaders. (Cook, 1977, p. vi)

Let's think about this situation and what it means. There is no reason why we—the educators who are working to become more professional—shouldn't know more and draw lessons from our local and our nation's literacy history. Our successes, our failures, our struggles, our triumphs should matter. We could advise policy-makers, institutional leaders, and fellow practitioners with greater insight if we could learn more lessons from our past; we could perhaps not be condemned to repeat mistakes, and perhaps we could realize what works in literacy for the future.

This chapter can get us thinking reflectively about our past. It can get us thinking about why we do what we do and where these traditions came from. And, it can help build a bridge to the next chapter, which is about personal philosophy toward adult education. As you read the following pages, you may want to think about the people being presented and consider if you think they are in fact "heroes and heroines." I have had at least one person argue that there is nothing "heroic about indoctrinating" learners about a singular ideology or religion, and many here were missionaries of some variety. Is that wrong? Are these heroes and heroines by today's standards? Are we entirely without some type of workplace imperative or social purpose when we teach in today's sponsor-driven literacy environment?

As you read this chapter, I suggest you consider the institutional and personal purposes at work in each landmark program presented, and consider the qualities of professionalism displayed by the founders and their co-workers. Then reflect on both with the chapter-end questions.

"TO RIGHT A WRONG": LITERACY AND SALVATION IN BRISTOL, ENGLAND, 1812

If someone were to point out that the history of reading and writing is far older than 1812—the starting point for this guide book—he or she would be quite right. Reading and writing date to the Village of Tell Brak, Syria about 4000 BCE in early Mesopotamia with the first known writing of the Sumerians (Fischer, 2003; Manguel, 1996). This is a long, complex history. However, as the research makes clear, the first documented, formalized, English-speaking adult school to teach reading that led to a lasting movement in the English-speaking world was the Bristol Institution for Instructing Adult Persons to Read the Holy Scriptures—or the Bristol Adult School, as it came to be called (Quigley, 2005; Verner, 1967). This is according to *Pole's History*, published in 1814 and reprinted by Verner in 1967. Here is the first history of adult education in the English-speaking world and the first place that the term "adult education" appeared in print (Hudson, 1969; Martin, 1924; Peers, 1972).

In Bristol, a port city on the Southwest coast of England, the first adult school had but one purpose. The Methodists wanted the adults in their city to read the Bible and, thereby, to be saved as Christian followers. However, in February 1812 something occurred that surprised the congregation: "During the second annual meeting of the local [Methodist] auxiliary of the Bible Society" (Martin, 1924, p. 26) at the Bristol Guild Hall, a letter was handed out explaining that some of the faithful who had been visited could not read. Therefore, what was the point of giving them Bibles? As Martin explained: "Not being able to read, [they] were unlikely to be benefited by possession of the Bible" (p. 26).

Simply ignoring those unable to read was not acceptable to William Smith, our first heroic figure in these historical landmarks. Smith is described as:

> a poor, humble, and almost unlettered individual . . . occupying no higher rank than that of a door-keeper to a Methodist chapel, without the slightest knowledge of what had been done in another province, [yet he] conceived the idea of instructing the adult poor to read the holy scriptures. (Hudson, 1969, p. 2, original printed 1851)

With the help of Stephen Prust, a "distinguished member of the Society of Friends" and local tobacco merchant ((Hudson, p. 3; Kelly, 1962), they set out to take names of those who might want to attend "a school for persons advanced in years" (Hudson, p. 3). On March 8, 1812, the first two adult learners to enter the room being rented for their school were William Wood, age 63, and Jane Burrace, age 40. Soon 11 men and 10 women followed "with the numbers increasing every week, until the rooms were filled" (p. 4). Later, Smith "engaged other apartments in the same neighborhood, for the reception and instruction of the illiterate poor, who were daily applying to him for admission" (p. 4).

In these humble beginnings we can see reflected the struggle for literacy resources endemic to literacy since. In fact, Smith "relinquished three shillings weekly from his small wages of eighteen shillings per week" (Hudson, p. 4) to cover expenses. We also see the beginnings of volunteerism and the driving force of compassion and commitment to those who simply seek to read. The very first initiative comes from ordinary people concerned for others, not from governments, not from the wealthiest, not from educational institutions. We see the beginning of a legacy being located in churches, civic centers, and schools un-used by children at night—not in buildings with the express purpose of teaching adult literacy. We see the notion that low literacy is somehow "temporary" and no more complicated than a few class meetings with good-hearted volunteers; and we see the beginning of social imperatives dictating the content of the curriculum. The Bristol program was not simply about reading, it was about reading the Bible. It was about internalizing its mes-sage both for individual salvation and to address community and national issues.

There are no written documents from Smith, Prust, or any of the original students, but Dr. Thomas Pole, their contempo-rary historian, explained in his 1814 history of this first Adult School movement that reading the Bible was of vital importance because "perusal of the sacred scripture and other religious books, have a tendency to moralize and Christianize the minds of men—instead of idleness, profaneness and vice—They incul-cate diligence, sobriety, frugality, piety, and heavenly-minded-ness" (Verner, 1967, p. 18, original published 1814).

Nowhere in *Pole's History* is there mention of learner needs—these will not part of the discussion until well into the 20th century. But there was a powerful argument about the bene-fits to be gained for England. In fact, through much of the 19th century it was assumed that access to the Scriptures would natu-rally lead to moral citizens and, subsequently, a more moral so-ciety. As Pole put it: "Industry, frugality, and economy will be their possession. They will also have learned better to practice meekness, Christian Fortitude, and resignation" (Verner, 1967, p. 19). As for England: "Once the good seed hath been sown . . . how changed will be the state of our fair isle! The lower classes will not then be so dependent on the provident members of society, as they now are" (p. 19).

The Bristol School movement was a huge success. In just one year, the Methodists' adult schools spread to Bath, Ipswich, Plymouth, Salisbury, and Yarmouth (Kelly, 1962, p. 150). The movement had grown to 21 schools by 1813, with 20 more added by 1815. The Society's annual report for 1816 showed

"24 schools for men and 31 for women, with a total member-
ship of 1,581 . . . [and adult schools] in Ireland, New York,
Philadelphia, and Sierra Leone" (Kelly, p. 150).

But there was a controversy brewing. Should they also be
teaching writing? These schools were typically held on Sundays,
and the Sabbath Day was to be held sacred with no work to be
conducted. Writing was deemed to be "work." Curiously, reading was never considered work—especially when reading the
Holy Bible. As a result, writing was rarely taught in these first
adult schools, and the issue became quite divisive among the
promoters.

But this may not have been the only reason not to teach
writing in this first school movement. In the early 1800s, the
illiterate and poor in England were typically feared as dangerous people of the lower classes. They were either criminals or
were seen as potential criminals—echoes of which can be seen
in some of the literacy readers used even today (Quigley &
Holsinger, 1993).

Many at the time actually wondered what the illiterate
poor would possibly want to write about. In fact, the prevailing
attitude was that teaching the lower classes to write would just
tempt them to commit forgery (Moore, 1997).

The Bristol Adult School movement and its Bible reading
programs were to become the formal model for the British colo-
nies. Of course, the United States was by then an independent
nation, but the American Missionary Association records, as
noted earlier, indicate that the Bristol Methodist mission was
also carried to America. One can see the imprint of the Bristol
Schools today in the sacrifice, passion, and zeal that drive many
in the field today. We also have the legacy of social imperatives
in the content used and ongoing political questions on "literacy
for what employment or social purpose?"

However one chooses to interpret our historical landmarks,
anyone who believes ours is a new field of practice; or believes
we have a benign, neutral, or perhaps a boring history; or assumes ours is a paler version of the public school's history,
(Cremin, 1964); or assumes the history of adult literacy takes
us back to ancient Mesopotamia, is quite mistaken.

Perhaps most important of all for purposes of building pride in this field of ours, the Bristol Movement shows us how educators and volunteers have stood up to make a difference in the face of what they saw as an injustice. Smith stood up out of compassion. He did so with personal courage despite what others might say. In all of our landmarks, we will see figures who struggled against all odds for what they believed was morally right in their time, including Rev. William Richardson who worked with the freed slaves of South Carolina, as seen next.

LITERACY FOR FREEDOM: THE PORT ROYAL EXPERIMENT, 1862–1865

It needs to be said that the complete history of adult literacy in Britain, Canada, and the United States is certainly not all about formal adult schools. Tom Sticht (2002) has given descriptive detail on examples of non-formal adult literacy education. Others, such as Harold Stubblefield and Patrick Keane (1994) have documented and interpreted a number of literacy events. For instance, there is research on the Puritans' very high levels of literacy and their absolute insistence on learning to read using the Bible. The children of the Puritans were taught to read with women teaching reading, men teaching math. Early missionaries to North America typically used informal literacy tutorial methods. Literacy tutoring on board navy ships was often conducted by the ship's medical doctor (Sticht). Parents taught their children by candlelight in prairie homesteads and in churches across North America using informal initiatives (Stubblefield & Keane). Attempting to find a way across the "top of the world" through the long-sought after North West Passage, some of the early Arctic explorers could not get their ships out before winter and were caught in the Arctic ice, sometimes for up to three years. This was the case with Capt. William Parry. The sailors were confined for months in the damp hold of the ship. Then, following the long dark winter of 1821, Parry stood and "beamed with pride as the sailors came up like bashful schoolchildren to present him with examples of their writing (Fleming, 1998, p. 11).

Parry later wrote this into his log book: "It is, I confess, with no ordinary feelings of pleasure that I record the fact that on the return of the Expedition to England, there was not an individual belonging to it who could not read his Bible" (cited in Fleming, p. 111; and see Berton, 1988).

Learning to read and write in what often were remarkable circumstances runs like a leitmotif through the early history of the United States and Canada. However, the first formalized, documented literacy program in English with a curriculum—and the first to receive federal funding support in the U.S. (Rachal, 1986)—making a lasting impact on adult literacy, took place at Port Royal, South Carolina. It occurred from 1862–1865 among the freed slaves of Port Royal.

When gun ships from the South Atlantic Blockading Squadron of the Union Army rounded the coastline and sailed into Port Royal Sound on November 7, 1861, they found that plantation owners, Confederate soldiers, and most residents of the South Carolina South Islands had fled. What General Thomas W. Sherman was greeted with was some 10,000 freed slaves standing in rags, many near starvation, and virtually all unable to read or write. Why were they illiterate? Because, to be a literate slave was actually illegal. In 1740, South Carolina became the first state to pass a law making it illegal to teach slaves to write and, in 1834, it also became illegal to teach slaves to read in South Carolina. Breaking these laws or the even harsher "plantation laws" in South Carolina, or those of the other Southern states that followed, had very serious consequences for the teacher and the learner. If caught, punishments could include having one's (writing) fingers chopped off, whippings, beatings, being branded with hot irons, or even being hanged (Quigley, 1987).

A few of the plantation slaves were highly numerate and had been allowed certain literacy skills since it was the lead slaves who effectively ran much of the day-to-day plantation operations. "House slaves" sometimes had higher literacy skills than their master's family due to the domestic and familial roles they were required to perform. But there were harsh punishments should they ever be caught teaching other slaves to read or write. Many did, nevertheless, and displayed acts of bravery unimaginable today (DeBoer, 1995).

In Port Royal, General Sherman was looking at an over-whelming set of social problems. He and his advisors undoubtedly had options, but they decided "to educate the freed slaves" (Stubblefield & Keane, 1994, pp. 130–131) and "recommended that Washington dispatch superintendents and instructors" (pp. 130–131). This was to become a huge social "experiment" for the North, in part because many Northerners were far from convinced that the freed slaves were even *capable* of learning, despite their belief that slavery was wrong (DeBoer, 1995).

Now appears on stage one of the long-forgotten literacy heroes of our field. Rev. William T. Richardson and members of the Gideonite religion answered the call for help and sailed from New York City March 3, 1862, under the auspices of the New York Freedmen's Relief Organization (an affiliate of the American Missionary Association, AMA). Despite whatever reactions one may have today to the idea of missionaries and colonization, Black leader Booker T. Washington saw such missionaries and literacy teachers as virtual saviors. He wrote: "Whenever it is written—and I hope it will be—the part that the Yankee teachers played in the education of the Negroes immediately after the war will make one of the most thrilling parts of the history of this country" (cited in DeBoer, 1995, Preface). W. E. B. DuBois, a major intellectual black leader and no supporter of white domination over African Americans, agreed that "the teachers came . . . not to keep Negroes in their place, but to raise them out of the places of defilement where slavery had sealed them" (cited in DeBoer, 1995, Preface).

Unlike the Bristol Movement, the teachers who came to Port Royal combined "religious and teaching instruction" (Rachal, 1986, p. 16); that is, their curriculum was both religious and secular. This religious-secular balance of content and motives continues through the century.

In the Port Royal area, new school buildings rose up. Thousands of freed slaves came forward. Both men and women, with the women often carrying their children on their hip or on their back as they walked for miles along dusty roads to reach the schools (Billington, 1953; Rachal, 1986). Deprived of reading and writing for generations, they came forward with "an instinctive sense of literacy's value" (Rachal, p. 16); fascinated, as Swint (1967) explains, with "that peculiar attraction which is characteristic of all forbidden fruit" (p. 72). Here was a revolution in learning, and an ominous rehearsal for the reconstruction that was to follow (Lovett, 1990).

Despite illnesses, endless work, and unimaginable struggle, Rev. William Richardson found time to write copious letters, "usually . . . by candlelight by screenless windows deep into the evening" (Rachal, 1986, p. 15). He mainly wrote to his superiors in New York about the progress being made while documenting the challenges and staggering frustrations he faced both in the Port Royal region and with the American Missionary Association itself. He often was pleading for further assistance. His wife joined him and worked by his side, as Richardson ultimately worked himself to death (American Missionary Association, 1868).

Significantly, the Richardsons took it as a secondary mission to address the ignorance and racial attitudes back home as they continually made it clear to a skeptical Northern audience there was no reason to doubt that these African American adult learners were their intellectual equals. The freed adults learned well and quickly. As Rachal (1986) points out, "In that context, Richardson's conclusion [on intelligence and ability] was ahead of its time" (p. 19).

However, not all literacy programs continue, especially when learning threatens the status quo. During reconstruction, a violent, relentless backlash arose from members of Southern slaveocracy who just would not tolerate slaves as free beings. In 1865, Francis Cardazo, Richardson's replacement, reported how the whites were filled with "hate and revenge toward the colored people," adding: "one thing especially provokes them . . . that is, our schools. . . . [They wish] to shut them up rather than see the colored people educated" (October 21, 1865, cited in Rachal, 1986). As historian W. J. Cash wrote in 1941, lynchings that "were unthinkable when blacks were valuable property, occurred with grisly regularity" after reconstruction began (cited in Rachal, p. 20).

Yet, even in the face of the cruelest forms of punishment and death, black men and women came forward in the thousands following the Civil War. It is an incredible chapter in American history, one that needs to be better known in our adult literacy field. Consider this event that occurred in Louisiana in 1864. According to the 1864 *Annual Report* of the American Missionary Association: "A most efficient system of education, [was] introduced into Louisiana by General Banks" (p. 24). Banks had placed a military tax on the entire population to support adult and child education for the Freedmen. Then, when the tax and the literacy programs were to be withdrawn, Superintendent Alvord of the Freedmens' Bureau reported the scene as follows:

> When the collection of the general tax for schools was suspended, the consternation of the colored population was intense. Petitions began to pour in. I saw one from the plantations across the river, at least thirty feet in length representing ten thousand negroes. It was affecting to examine it, and note the names and marks (x) [sic] of such a long list of parents, ignorant themselves but begging that their children might be educated; promising that, from beneath their present burdens, and out of their extreme poverty, they would pay for it. (p. 24)

Consider the dedication of Miss Wells, a recent graduate of Mount Holyoke, who "followed the army before peace was declared into one of the bitterest and most conservative parts of the South" (Congregational Milestones, cited in DeBoer, 1995, p. 119). She opened her school in Athens, Alabama. Shortly thereafter: "The Ku Klux Klan lined up around her school, fired volleys of shot . . . through her windows on either side of the chair on which was sitting" (cited in DeBoer, p. 119). Threats continued until "the school was burned down over her head" (p. 119). At this point, the American Missionary Association urged her to come home. Instead, Miss Wells "established a brick yard, set the negroes to making bricks, and under her direction they built the school house which served them for many years" (cited in DeBoer, p. 119). The stories are many. Harriet Jacobs, once a slave herself, helped create the famous Freedmen's Schools following the Civil War. The history of our field is filled with heroic figures—teachers and learners alike.

But what have we learned from the struggles of teachers and programs over the past century and a half? Why not document our own local, regional, and national stories? Remember, even these Civil War stories and the others here are the history as described by those who could write it and with the influence to have their writing disseminated or preserved. Our learners remain silent in most of the records of adult literacy. We could change that. Also, we know little of the untold stories of those exceptional governmental officials, politicians, and community leaders who have played a vital role in our struggle (Akenson & Neufeldt, 1990; Quigley, 1997).

We lack heroes and heroines in our field. If only we knew more—cared more—about our own history, I believe we would be less willing to accept of the deficit perspective and images that so often depict this "temporary" field of ours in the media, the literature, in the policy-based descriptions of our field. And— although I hate to add it—in our own recruitment materials in many cases (Quigley, 1997).

"WHEREVER AND WHENEVER": CANADA'S FRONTIER COLLEGE, 1899 TO TODAY

While Freedmen walked miles to the adult schools of Port Royal, Frontier College took literacy to learners. Even after over 100 years, Frontier College still takes literacy to the remotest corners of Canada and, in recent years, it has also been going to the "frontiers" of city streets with programs where street people help others who are homeless with their literacy skills. Frontier College was established on the vision of Alfred Fitzpatrick. As Fitzpatrick stated in 1920: "Wherever and whenever [people] have occasion to gather, then and there shall be the time, place and means of their education" (cited in Krotz, 1999, p. v).

Fitzpatrick was born in the farming community of Mills-

Figure A-1 Alfred Fitzpatrick, Founder of Frontier College.
Simpson Brothers/Library and Archives Canada/C-056817.

ville, Pictou County, Nova Scotia, Canada, in 1862. The second youngest of 12 children (Morrison, 1989), Alfred grew up knowing that one older brother, Lee, had worked and died in the redwood lumber camps of California. He also saw Isaac, another older brother, leave for the same redwood forests to work, and the family had not heard from him since. After graduating in 1892 with a degree in theology to become a Presbyterian minister, Fitzpatrick decided to serve as a missionary to the workers

Figure A-2 D. L. McDougall teaching civics to a class of Scandinavian adults at a nickel mine in Northern Ontario, Canada, 1913. *Simpson Brothers/Library and Archives Canada/PA-06177.*

Figure A-3 Frontier College instructor Neal Grant's reading tent in the interior of British Columbia, Canada, 1911. C-057063.

in lumber camps. In his search of one lost brother and for the gravesite of another, it was "in the towering forests of California that Fitzpatrick was to define his life work" (p. 5).

According to oral history, Fitzpatrick was working as a minister in a California lumber camp and one day accidentally met his long-lost brother, Isaac. The story goes that Alfred recognized Isaac immediately, but Isaac, having been away for 20 years at that point, did not recognize Alfred. Alfred offered his older brother a lift in his wagon, and "It was during this drive through the majestic evergreens" (Morrison, p. 6) that Isaac learned he was reunited with the brother he assumed was some 4,000 miles away. As they talked, the stories Isaac told about the brutal work life in the lumber camps and the complete lack of workers' recourse to a union, a church, or a governmental agency, led Alfred to resolve "to devote his life to those who laboured on the frontier" (p. 6).

At the turn of the 20th century, there was a growing number of social and reformist philanthropists, charities, church groups, and governmental agencies that helped the marginalized and working poor in Canadian towns and cities, but there was little help for the thousands working beyond society's urban and rural centers. These were the forgotten who worked in Canada's mines, remote lumber camps, and the railway steel gangs that moved across the vast expanses of Canada. As Morrison states: "Their working conditions were appalling, their living conditions primitive" (p. 7).

Fitzpatrick worked from the prevailing Social Gospel reform movement at the turn of the century. For Fitzpatrick, this meant that knowledge was "the God-given right of every person, not the exclusive privilege of the favoured few" (Morrison, p. 8). He began his reformist work in a lumber camp near Nairn Centre in Northern Ontario in 1899 and set up his first reading camp in October 1900. As other young university graduates followed, they managed to establish 24 reading rooms in log structures or canvas tents in various locations throughout this Northern region. The young university volunteers—mainly young males— were financially supported by church donations, private, commercial, and some governmental support. They taught the workers in the evenings when the workers' day was over. The teaching model evolved into one where the volunteers, still called labourer-teachers, no longer sat waiting for the workers to return. Instead, they worked shoulder-to-shoulder with them all day, and then taught literacy to those who came to the reading tent, box car, or construction hut at night. The labourer-teachers today still work for the same wages as their learners, still do the same work as their learners, and still find the stamina to teach literacy in the evenings just as they have for over a century.

Fitzpatrick took a Social Gospel educationist's approach. That is, he did not fight to unionize workers, bring about socialist, or political reform. His way was to seek individual change through education, not systemic change through radical reform. This individualism approach was attractive to the Canadian government, which supported his efforts. By 1920, the labourer-teacher ranks had grown to 46 men and 3 women. Fitzpatrick personally wrote the *Handbook for New Canadians* in 1919, and "Each instructor was sent to the frontier grasping a volume to promote Canadianism" (Morrison, 1989, p. 13). Translations of 700 words of Italian, French, Swedish, Ukrainian, and Yiddish into English were added to "materials on Canada's history and government, naturalization, and basic English language structure" (p. 13). By 1920, some 100,000 workmen had been taught by over 500 labourer-teachers.

In 1919, degree-granting authority was granted to the college but, to Fitzpatrick's dismay, the charter would never be fulfilled. Like several of these landmark programs, there often comes a point where successful literacy programs inevitably clash with the status quo of education. In this case, most of the largest universities, colleges, and provincial departments of education across Canada would not accept such a sweeping "national college." The idea threatened their dominance within provincial regions, and raised numerous questions about jurisdictions and power. Despite every effort by Fitzpatrick and a stellar Board of Examiners that included some of Canada's most lauded scholars, ultimately, despite the charter, "little or no financial support was forthcoming from [the same] government" (Morrison, 1989, p. 15).

Fitzpatrick died in 1925 along with his dream of a degree-granting institution. Edmund Bradwin continued as president, doing what Frontier College had always done best, placing labourer-teachers throughout the frontiers of Canada as a volunteer, *non-credit* undertaking. By 1967, the number of labourer-teachers was 72, with half of those in railway work, a quarter in the mines, and the remaining quarter in logging camps. Today, labourer-teachers work alongside migrant workers on farms and in market gardens, and many others have taken white-collar work roles. Frontier College is reaching new frontiers among the physically and mentally challenged in literacy, it is building learning partnerships with Canada's Native People, with prison literacy and the promotion of reading with young people. The original concept of taking literacy to the people remains alive and well with Frontier College. Fitzpatrick's philosophy of working with the oppressed "whenever and wherever they are" is still at work in Canadian literacy today; and, it weathered the threat that innovative literacy programs often seemed to pose to other established institutions. Through time, according to researcher Pierre Walter (personal communication), there has been a perceived shift from social gospel to a social justice orientation in Frontier College, from helping individuals, specifically, to working with them and advocating for them in the face of systemic injustices. Here is a longstanding point of ideological difference among programs in field of adult literacy and basic education.

What model is in fact best if we are to be effective literacy educators? Compare Frontier College's approach with the landmark programs to follow.

"HUMBLE BUT OFFICIAL BEGINNINGS" IN THE U.S.A.: THE MOONLIGHT SCHOOLS OF KENTUCKY, 1911

At the turn of the 20th century, Rowan County was considered the poorest county in Kentucky. Despite the countless obstacles, the countless skeptics, and despite having no funds whatsoever, in 1911 Cora Wilson Stewart opened the doors of the Little Brushy schoolhouse in Rowan County to adult learners (Baldwin, 2005). Here was a female in a male-dominated

Figure B-1 Cora Wilson Stewart, Founder of the Moonlight Schools of Kentucky.
Negatives Courtesy of Yvonne Baldwin Photographs at Margaret King Library, University of Kentucky and online at <http://kdl.kyv.org>.

society with few precedents, few mentors to draw on, repeatedly being told that her undertaking was doomed to failure because "elderly folks were too self-conscious and embarrassed to go to night school" (Taylor, 1973, p. 23). She hoped that perhaps 150 adults would come forward. Instead, 1,200 enrolled in the first year. Incredibly, 1,600 enrolled the second, and by 1913 no fewer than 25 counties had established Moonlight Schools for adult learners (Baldwin, 2005). Four years after Stewart had opened those doors of the Little Brushy one-room schoolhouse, Alabama had established "Adult Schools" (Taylor, 1973, p. 24); South Carolina "Lay-By Schools"; the Community Schools appeared in North Carolina; and "Schools for Grown-Ups" were

Figure B-2 An adult education night class being held in one of the "moonlight schools."
Negatives courtesy of Yvonne Baldwin Photographs at Margaret King Library, University of Kentucky and online at <http://kdl.kyv.org>.

Figure B-3 Elderly students of moonlight school movement holding their Bible.
Negatives courtesy of Yvonne Baldwin Photographs at Margaret King Library, University of Kentucky and online at <http://kdl.kyv.org>.

created in Georgia. All of these were based on the Kentucky model (Taylor, 1973, pp. 24–25). By 1914, Oklahoma had not only established its version but offered credit in its Normal Schools for those teachers who had taught in the adult education schools. In 1915, Washington State created adult night schools on the Kentucky model, as did Minnesota and New Mexico. Today we have "night schools" and literacy programs for adults across North America. Cora Wilson Stewart's hand helped form the pattern for what we see and what we do across North America today. Yet few know her name.

Her idea was simple enough. If the moon was shining, it was a signal to adults anywhere that they were welcome to come down from the hills and up from the valleys to learn to read and write in the local schoolhouses. The lessons were then carried in the local *Rowan County Messenger*. Besides being school superintendent and holding various other responsible positions, including principal of two schools at one point, Stewart was the editor of the local newspaper.

Nicknamed "the General" by her father (Estes, 1988, p. 115), at age 15 she began teaching in the Morehead Public School, and her students included her own brothers and sisters. Between school sessions, she attended the National Normal University in Lebanon, Ohio, and continued her education at the Morehead Normal School and the State University of Kentucky (Taylor, 1973, p. 27). But it was adult illiteracy that became her life's work. By her own account, three incidents led her to focus on adult literacy. A mother asked her for help to write to a daughter who had recently moved to Chicago. A middle-aged man "with tears in his eyes," (Mandrell, n.d., p. 14) begged to be helped to learn to read and write so he could feel "whole." And an aspiring local musician who could not write and could therefore not pursue his dreams asked Wilson for help. These three events turned her from teaching children to teaching adults (By the light, 2001).

Besides establishing the movement, she wrote the program's first teaching materials, including the *Country Life Readers* and later *The Prisoner's First Book* for the state. She was named to the Kentucky Illiteracy Commission in 1914—a commission she herself had proposed—and later became its chairperson. Years ahead of her time, Stewart included Native Indians and African American adults in the literacy movement. During World War I, she was asked to be the advisor the U.S. army on adult literacy. She wrote *The Soldier's First Book* so the thousands of soldiers with low literacy skills could write home and, in turn, read the letters sent to them.

On a personal level, she gave birth to one child who died in less than a year. Her first husband, Alexander Stewart, was a schoolteacher who is recorded in the research as a chronic alcoholic "who verbally and physically abused" her (Estes, 1988, p. 117), to the point that local court records show that Cora had to flee her home on several occasions and take refuge with friends in Morehead. According to Estes, "Alex's violence and threats grew in intensity and frequency until, in March 1910, he drew a pistol and aimed it at her, but the gun misfired. Shortly thereafter, Wilson was granted a divorce" (p. 117). Nevertheless, through this same period, she managed to hold two principals' positions as well as establish the moonlight schools.

Cora Wilson Stewart was a national leader in adult literacy during World War I. She was named chair of the Illiteracy Commission of the National Education Association in 1919 and in 1923 chair of the World Illiteracy Commission "and presided over conferences in Edinburgh, Geneva, Toronto, San Francisco, and Denver" (Taylor, 1973, p. 25). The first National Illiteracy Crusade in the U.S.A. was conducted in 1924 under *New York Times* Editor John H. Finley. It had no evident successes. Then in 1926 President Calvin Coolidge named Stewart director of his National Illiteracy Crusade and also appointed her as director of the new National Illiteracy Commission using the very model that had its beginnings in Rowan County just 15 short years earlier. Under Stewart's leadership, Americanization and what would later be ESL programs for new immigrants were included in literacy programming, as were "illiterate groups of Indians and Blacks" (Cook, 1977, p. 31) across the United States.

But literacy programs always seem to come up against the status quo. Despite her Herculean efforts and almost two decades of success on the world stage, in 1920 a bill before the Kentucky legislature for $75,000 to continue her work was defeated. Fifty-seven of the 120 county superintendents in Kentucky were surveyed for their support. They chose not to support the Moonlight Schools. Instead some chose to personally attack Stewart (Baldwin, 2005). Clearly threatened by the success of the Moonlight Schools and the implicit criticism it was making on their own less-than-successful school system, the superintendents argued for more funding to their schools, none for adults. Some called the entire movement "a fad and a failure" (cited in Estes, 1988, p. 251). Other superintendents insisted Stewart should "channel her effort" elsewhere (cited in Estes, p. 251). Her heroic successes recognized around the world were locally deemed "Quixotic." Wilson continued her work, but on December 1958, she died in relative obscurity at age 61 in a North Carolina nursing home.

Like Richardson and William Smith before her, the compassion and strength of one person made an enormous difference, but the politics of literacy are far less compassionate. The singular struggle, the personal sacrifices, the voluntary nature of literacy, the use of school buildings and churches after hours, the public assumption that adult literacy is some sort of educational "anomaly," the myth that adults won't come forward— just so many social stereotypes and systemic injustices have become normalized today.

Are things really so different now? Where is the permanent infrastructure for adult literacy and basic education after a century of struggle? Why do we live on "grants?" What could we all be doing differently to establish literacy as a true educational system along side all the other educational systems we now take for granted? The next story gives food for thought, since it turns literacy from individualism to social reform and wide public awareness.

LITERACY FOR DEMOCRACY: HULL HOUSE, 1889

Jane Addams remains as one of America's best known heroines, even if she is not often recognized as a leader in adult literacy. A founder of Hull House—one of the most famous examples in the Settlement House movement established to help immigrants in the late 19th and early 20th century—Addams challenged many 19th-century conventions, including attitudes towards poverty, democracy, and reasons for illiteracy. She came to believe that her mission was to *reform society*, not *individuals*. As Davis (1973) explained: "Jane Addams never became a radical in religion, in economics, or in politics, but she did become a social reformer, a defender of organized labor, and she did come to believe that *her main task was to eliminate poverty rather than to comfort the poor* [italics added]" (p. 74).

Addams grew to believe that "blaming the victim," an attitude endemic to Western society then (and now), was wrong-headed. That view was simply too dismissive, too self-serving, and too easy. Problems of poverty and low literacy "flow from social causes," she said (Diliberto, 1999, p. 254).

Born into a wealthy family, Addams first attended the Rockford Seminary near her family home in northern Illinois. She was being encouraged by her teachers to follow a life of service, but instead she read extensively and came to favor the "ideal of mingled learning, piety, and physical labor, more exemplified by the Port Royalists than by any others" (Ferris, 1943, pp. 198–199). Here we see the power of literacy carried through our literacy landmarks.

Although she had a sheltered upbringing and had seen poverty in Rockford, it was the urban squalor and destitution of the men, women, and children she saw during her educational tours of Europe, especially in the East End of London, southern Italy, and Austria, that drew her to become "convinced that it would be a good thing to rent a house in a part of the city [of Chicago] where many primitive and actual needs are found" (Ferris, 1943, p. 219).

With Brenda Starr Gates, her life-long friend and companion, Jane Addams took up residence on September 18, 1889, on the first floor of a house formerly belonging to the Hull family on South Halstead Street, the heart of Chicago's most oppressive slums. Their organization's charter of incorporation read: "To provide a center for a higher civic and social life; to institute and maintain educational and philanthropic enterprises, and to

Figure C-1 Jane Addams, founder of Hull House, was awarded the Nobel Peace Prize in 1931.
Jane Addams Memorial Special Collection Department. University Library, University of Chicago. JAMC—negative #1167.

Figure C-2 Immigrants lived in squalor in the slums around Hull House.
Jane Addams Memorial Special Collection Department. University Library, University of Chicago. JAMC—negative #275.

Figure C-3 Miss Ball teaching a citizenship class in the Hull House complex.
Jane Addams Memorial Special Collection Department. University Library, University of Chicago. JAMC—negative #1839

investigate and improve the conditions in the industrial districts of Chicago" (Linn, 1935, p. 110). They were soon joined by other women, including Julia Lathrop and Florence Kelley (Linn).

Due to the women's family connections, they were able to connect with some of Chicago's most influential families. Their Settlement House became something of a bridge to the nation's upper classes. Philanthropists, intellectuals, artists, and politicians became part of their cause. The women effectively had a dual role. They educated the upper classes of Chicago and much of America, along with the poorest in the Hull House area. We carry a similar "dual role" today. What was very different from today was that adults flocked to their programs. Incredibly, "some 50,000 people . . . came to the House" (Linn, p. 115) and "the second year the number increased to 2,000 per week" (p. 115).

It is fascinating to see where they put their first efforts. Where would they begin in this sea of squalor? Educated in literature and the arts, the Hull House women began a discussion and reading group for young women. They offered courses on Dante and Browning to the immigrant working women in the area, and then "other residents led Shakespeare and Plato clubs" (Bryan, Bair, & DeAngury, 2003, p. 549). The Working People's Social Science Club was created, and speakers such as John Dewey and Susan B. Anthony visited Hull House. They created a lending library of books and framed photographs of master paintings, even delivering them to the tenement houses. They established a biannual exhibit of works of art and encouraged the "Chicago matrons . . . to loan artwork from their private collections" (p. 550).

But faced with appalling health, unemployment, and living conditions in an area where children were playing with rats as pets and families were dying of diseases brought on by garbage and raw sewage in the streets, the women of Hull House turned more and more to projects that might alleviate poverty conditions. Art classes were transformed into craft-making courses. A book bindery workshop was attempted. Dressmaking courses and millinery courses thrived. A Boy's Club was opened with shops to teach "work in wood, iron, and brass . . . copper and tin; . . . commercial photography, printing, telegraphy, and electrical construction" (Lagemann, 1985, p. p. 179). A public kitchen to teach cooking and provide nutritious American meals was opened (but largely failed since many immigrants in the area would not cook or eat such "foreign food"). They helped with birthing, washing and preparing the dead, helping in every aspect of people's struggle to survive. But they increasingly realized it was not enough.

Addams and her colleagues came to see how power rested in the hands of a small number of Chicago's wealthiest. At the time, the suggestion of an eight-hour work day "was connected in the minds of many employers not only with laziness but directly with anarchy, the blackest word in the vocabulary of the governing minority" (Linn, 1935, p. 101). Hull House is today credited with helping to initiate the Factory Acts so the children of America could no longer be so exploited.

With her colleagues, Addams fought for women's suffrage. Brenda Starr Gates marched for union rights. Addams became the first woman president of the National Conference on Social Work, the founder and first president of the National Federation of Settlements, the national chair of the Women's Peace Party, and the president and co-founder of the Women's International League for Peace and Freedom. She was awarded the Nobel Peace Prize in 1931 and ended her life as one of America's greatest champions of the poor and oppressed.

Despite her international recognition and her Nobel Peace Prize, it was her lifelong fight to place the responsibility for the appalling conditions of impoverished immigrants unable to read or write in the English language at the doorstep of the magnates of industry and corrupt politicians. Hers was a fight for democracy. This meant literacy education. She is remembered for Americanization classes, ESL classes, basic literacy and basic education, and a vast range of vocational and arts-based programs and venues with a vision of dignity and opportunity for all. What also should be remembered, and discussed, is how Addams and her colleagues moved from the prevailing "blame the victim" perspective that said every individual could succeed in America's meritocracy if he or she really wanted, to a determination to achieve social justice. Rather than the individual, they came to see that external forces and systemic power imbalances were the primary cause of oppression, poverty, and illiteracy for individuals.

Significantly, literacy was not the raison d'être of Hull House. It was a single element in the vocational, cultural, and social change mission of these women. And here is another important pattern. Literacy and basic education in North America has an unquestionable legacy of women, not only taking leadership but being the mainstay of this field. If women had not chosen to step forward for well over a century, the high numbers of adults with low literacy skills that policy-makers decry today would be infinitely higher.

But our strengths are often our weaknesses. It has been well argued that the literacy field is one of the clearest examples of female exploitation in all of education (Luttrell, 1996; Quigley, 1997). Wendy Luttrell has pointed out that "Women are concentrated in literacy instruction, particularly as volunteers or as part-time instructors with little or no pay, job mobility or career advancement" (p. 343). The public attitude, she says with sarcasm, is that women should naturally be "taking care of literacy" (p. 343). Literacy is assumedly some sort of extension of "mothering." As this argument goes, the sacrifices by women have become so "normalized" that they are simply expected.

The next vignette takes us one step farther into a community development approach based on families and entire communities. Across the Canadian maritime provinces, literacy was again but one of the tools used by women, men, and children working together with other families to build a new future.

"KNOWLEDGE FOR THE PEOPLE": THE ANTIGONISH MOVEMENT, 1931

We end where we began—with religious figures. But for Father Moses Coady and Father Jimmy Tompkins, Catholic priests living on the North Atlantic coast of Nova Scotia in eastern Canada, literacy was not a vehicle to salvation, or even to Catholicism. Here learners had perhaps the strongest voice yet in the decisions that would affect their lives. And as might have been noted to this point, the roots of adult literacy have grown not from learners' expressed needs but society's cultural, religious, and political imperatives (Arnove & Graff, 1987).

According to historians Selman et al., the Antigonish Movement is today "the most famous adult education project in Canada and the best known outside our borders" (1998, p. 45). Taking its name from the small university town of Antigonish, the movement arose from a long history of dependence on the

Figure D-1 Moses Coady was a tireless speaker in establishing the Antigonish Movement.
Courtesy St. Francis Xavier Archives Collection: Extension Department Collection Conf. #89-568-633.

fishing industry throughout northern Nova Scotia and its neighboring provinces. In addition, these maritime provinces had been the center of wooden ship building for Canada and had a long history of trade with the "Boston States." But "the golden age of wind and sail" was waning by the turn of the century and was well over by the 1920s. The jobs along with the population had declined. Thriving industries and employment fell away to

Figure D-2 Many Nova Scotia fishing villages were kept in poverty by large fishing companies.
Courtesy St. Francis Xavier Archives Collection: National Film Board Collection #89-568-413.

such an extent that this once prosperous region came to be called "the graveyard of industry" (Coady, cited in Welton, 2001, p. 48). The fishermen and their families were effectively owned by the remaining conglomerates. The "companies" owned the fishing boats and gear, and the annual catch of every fisherman went to pay the "advances" of the past year. Fishermen would often end the season owing more to the fishery companies than when they began.

Coal miners lived an equally feudal existence in dilapidated houses owned by the mine owners. All miners were compelled to deal in the company stores. Work conditions were medieval. In the beautiful rural countryside, farmers worked to eke out an existence by taking their products to markets again owned by companies, which not only had the marketing resources but also the knowledge of "the outside world." The few steel mills that

Figure D-3 Mary Arnold helped adults in Nova Scotia learn about housing construction.
Courtesy St. Francis Xavier Archives Collection: Extension Department Collection Conf. #89-567-722.

made up the industries of Cape Breton exploited child labor in conditions at least as dangerous as those found in Chicago or other industrialized cities in the Northeastern states.

One clergyman in Nova Scotia reported that families in his district "were living on 4 cents a day . . . [and] children were clothed in discarded flour bags and . . . the only bedclothes were old feed bags" (cited in Welton, 2001, p. 45). In late December 1925, after visiting the coal regions, the bishop of the Antigonish Diocese wrote a letter to all the priests in his diocese saying he had "direct evidence that there is a large number of people who are [on] the verge of starvation" (cited in Welton, p. 45). He urged the clergy to do whatever they could.

Two priests from the small university town of Antigonish did indeed do something. With the help of many organizers and the work of thousands of men and women, within a decade the economy of the entire region was turning around and the dignity of thousands was restored. Beginning in the 1920s, the movement came to include the provinces of Nova Scotia, New Brunswick, Prince Edward Island, and to a lesser extent, Newfoundland. It was at its peak from the early 1930s to the 1940s and continued into the 1950s. Its traditions can still be seen in the local region and university today. Adult education was the vehicle they used for independence and self-reliance, but it is important to see the part literacy played.

Father Jimmy Tompkins had been on the faculty of the local university, St. Francis Xavier University, in Antigonish. An avid reader and visionary, Tompkins published and distributed a pamphlet in 1921 entitled *Knowledge for the People*. It advocated "useful knowledge" as the key to the flagging regional economy. He urged the community to begin to share their labor and their products. He urged his university colleagues at St. Francis Xavier University "to go out to the people" (Alexander, 1997, p. 68). In the same year, the first People's School was held at St. Francis Xavier and subjects such as economics, mathematics, agriculture, and public speaking were taught to the fishermen, farmers, and laborers who came forward. But, as Tompkins insisted, it was too centralized, too textbook-based. The university decided to establish an Extension Department in 1930 under the direction of Father Moses Coady. Highly influenced by Father Jimmy Tompkins, the Antigonish Movement was born (Lotz, 2005).

Its stated mission was: "The improvement of the economic, social, educational and religious condition of the people of eastern Nova Scotia" (cited in Alexander, 1997, p. 78). Coady traveled tirelessly to town after town speaking in town halls, churches, anywhere he could assemble a public meeting. He talked of creating cooperatives, sharing resources, pooling energies, marketing products directly. Above all, he encouraged the people to stand up for themselves. They did not have to be "slaves to company owners." Coady did not begin with classes on literacy. Instead, study clubs were created in community after community, each provided with literature to read. Communities were to think about and discuss the issues, to consider possible solutions to their situation by combining their own labor and imagination.

Importantly, despite the fact that Coady was acutely aware of the question of illiteracy, grassroots adult education movement did not mean structured literacy or basic education classes in this movement. Instead, neighbors helped neighbors in the study clubs as they read and discussed the pamphlets and materials provided by the St. Francis Xavier Extension Department, and by Father Coady on his frequent visits. Friends helped friends, families helped families. They identified their problems and got on with the job. Literacy was a vehicle on the road, not a destination unto itself.

In 1930–31, the first full year of the Extension Department's operation, a total of 192 general meetings were held with 14,856 people attending. One-hundred seventy-three study clubs had been created with 1,384 members by 1931. By 1935, there were 940 clubs with 10,650 participants, and 84 cooperatives or credit unions were in place making small business loans to members. By 1938, less than a decade after it began, 10,000 members belonged to the Antigonish Movement—a remarkable number for a sparsely populated region with many communities accessible only by boat.

From these study clubs, gatherings, and the oratory of Moses Coady, communities created credit unions so fishermen, farmers, steel workers, and miners could get small loans and begin to own their own fishing equipment; miners began to organize for better wages; farmers began to take their products directly to market. Some villages and towns undertook to build houses using a cooperative housing approach—always under the scornful eye of local builders who claimed every house would fall down.

Above all—quite literally "above all" since he towered at over six feet—Father Moses Coady stood using his transfixing oratory to turn despair into hope (Welton, 2001). Coady addressed the United Nations in August 1949 on "Organizing Rural People for the Proper Use and Conservation of Natural Resources." He became a force across parts of the U.S. and throughout Eastern Canada as he spoke indefatigably to cooperative movements and philanthropist organizations, to anyone who would share the vision. But his dreams, according to biographer Michael Welton, ultimately could only take people so far. The "new, permanent cooperative order" (Welton, p. 217) he preached and lived, never fully appeared. The world-wide, permanent new order he dreamed of was never realized. After a series of heart problems and illnesses, he collapsed at the microphone addressing a cooperative rally in Wisconsin. He died July 28, 1959, in St. Martha's Hospital in Antigonish, Nova Scotia. His casket was carried to its final resting place in the local Antigonish cemetery by a steelworker, a coal miner, two farmers, and two fishermen.

His life's philosophy was that people can create their own answers by building upon family and community strength. They can be "masters of their own destiny," to use Coady's famous phrase.

I now live in the Antigonish community myself and teach at St. Francis Xavier. Our faculty Department of Adult Education is the same building used by the original Extension Department. My office is near the one Coady worked in and often slept in, as he worked around the clock. People like Moses Coady, Jimmy Tompkins, and the workers in the famous Extension Department are far from forgotten. International seminars and conferences are regularly held on issues of development and globalization, and the Coady International Institute on the St. Francis Xavier campus works with more than 50 developing countries to teach cooperative adult education practices. Just a few blocks from where I live, there are houses—yes, still standing—constructed during the Antigonish Movement.

People ask why the Antigonish Movement isn't still alive today working with those who still need help in this same region. I wish I had an answer. And here is a vital question for all who care about the future of our field. Why, with this range of program models to learn from, and with the numerous examples of personal courage to draw upon, has no industrialized nation eradicated illiteracy? Or let's begin at home. I am a board member of our local community-based adult literacy organization. We are still looking for the funding to pay this year's rent. Why?

CHAPTER 2 DISCUSSION TOPICS FOR CONSIDERATION IN YOUR LEARNING JOURNAL AND LEARNING CIRCLE

Write your reflections on this chapter and on the following questions in your journal. Then, discuss them with your learning circle.

- Is there a zeal or passion in your program today similar to those seen in this chapter? What does the commitment in your program look like? That is, what are some examples of personal commitment? Why do people in your program do this work?
- Why do you think some adult schools and adult literacy programs have survived for years and others fail to survive?
- Who made the decisions on what the learning content and purposes of adult literacy should be in each of these landmarks? Who makes them for your program?
- We saw salvationist reform for individuals in the early programs, and commitment for social justice in the later ones. Is your program involved more with individuals and individual change, or more with social and community change? Should the balance be different?
- What lessons for program survival can be learned from these stories?
- Looking at the content and intentions of these programs through today's eyes, were these programs about ideological or religious "indoctrination?"
- Do you think everyone is agreed on the same purposes for your program? Do you have a written mission statement of purpose for your program? What role should learners play in these decisions?
- If you were to name three reasons why your program has con-

tinued and give some advice to new programs on how to survive and flourish, what would that advice be?

- What role did professionalism play in the stories of these landmarks?
- What are your thoughts on the role women have played in this
history?
- Why do you think literacy history is so absent from the literacy literature? Why is it not a larger part of policy decisions,
both locally and federally?
- Please enter any further thoughts you have about this chapter
in your journal, and discuss those points you are comfortable
discussing in your learning circle.

CHAPTER 2
ACTIVITY OPTIONS FOR FOLLOW-UP

Local History and Local Practice

Has anyone ever documented the history of your program or
conducted audio/video interviews with some of the founders,
teachers, or learners? If not, take on this local history project,
possibly with the help of some of your learners.

1) If you take on this project, what lessons are there for your
program today? Is your program very different from when it
was begun? How did the early practitioners in your program
recruit learners? How did they deal with dropouts? How did
they recruit teachers and tutors? How did they support the
program? How did they keep enthusiasm high for the program in the community and region? What were the earliest
challenges to survival and success; are they different today?

2) Try to put a history together on the creation and establishment of adult literacy education in your area, perhaps with
some of the other providers. Could this be printed for all new
practitioners, students, or policy-makers? Imagine a book
with photos and interviews in it. Or an attractive Website of
the history of adult literacy in your community. Imagine it act-

ing as a guide for others on what works best in your own area.

Looking at Your Own Program

3) If you don't already have one, try writing a mission statement for your program. What are its purpose(s) and goals? Try writing it in your learning journal first, and then look back at it after the next chapter on working philosophy. People often have very different ideas about the appropriate purposes for literacy programs—as the early history of adult literacy in this chapter suggests. You may want to re-think questions of social justice and individualism having read this chapter, or you may want to introduce some new objectives in your classroom as a result of reading and discussing the next chapter.

4) What are some stories from the learners of your program through time? Can you document some of these stories in written form, or with audio interviews to create an oral history? Imagine this being an entry guide for new students to your program today. What did earlier students fear? Struggle with? And accomplish?

5) Do you think the major figures in these landmarks were "professionals"? Were the heroes and heroines of your early programs "professionals"? Why or why not?

Any further thoughts you have on history, professionalism, and literacy should be entered in your journal and consider discussing them with your learning friends.

CHAPTER 2: FURTHER READING

On The Bristol School

Martin, C. (1924). *The adult school movement*. London: National Adult School Union.

Peers, R. (1972). *Adult education: A comparative study*. London: Routledge & Kegan Paul.

Verner, C. (Ed.). (1967). *Pole's history of adult schools*. Washington, DC: Adult Education Associates in the U.S.A. (Original work by T. Pole published 1814).

On Port Royal and Early Adult Literacy in the Southern States

Akenson, J. E., & Neufeldt, H. G. (1990). The Southern literacy campaign for Black adults in the early twentieth century. In H. G. Neufeldt, & L. McGee (Eds.), *Education of the African American adult* (pp. 179–190). Westport, CT: Greenwood Press.

DeBoer, C. M. (1995). *His truth is marching on: African Americans who taught the freed men for the American Missionary Association, 1861–1877*. New York: Garland Publishing.

Rachal, J. R. (1986). Freedom's crucible: William T. Richardson and the schooling of freed men. *Adult Education Quarterly, 1*(37), 14–22.

On Frontier College

Morrison, J. H. (1989). *Camps & classrooms: A pictorial history of Frontier College*. Toronto: The Frontier College Press.

Selman, G., Selman, M., Cooke, M., & Dampier, P. (1998). *The foundations of adult education in Canada*, 2nd ed. Toronto: Thompson Educational Publishing.

On the Moonlight Schools of Kentucky

Baldwin, Y. H. (2005). *Cora Wilson Stewart and the Moonlight Schools: Fighting for literacy in Kentucky*. Lexington: University Press of Kentucky.

Estes, F. (1988). *Cora Wilson Stewart and the moonlight*

schools Kentucky, 1911–1920. A case study in the rhetorical uses of literacy. Unpublished doctoral dissertation, The University of Kentucky, Lexington.

On Jane Addams and Hull House

Davis, A. F. (1973). *American heroine: The life and legend of Jane Addams.* New York: Oxford University Press.

Linn, J. W. (1935). *Jane Addams: A biography.* New York: D. Appleton-Century.

On the Antigonish Movement

Coady, M. M. (1939). *Masters of their own destiny.* New York: Harper and Brothers.

Lotz, J. (2005). The humble giant: Moses Coady, Canada's rural revolutionary. Ottawa, Canada: Novalis.

Welton, M. R. (2001). *Little Mosie from the Margaree: A biography of Moses Michael Coady.* Toronto: Thompson Education Publishing.

CHAPTER 3

"Why Do We Teach?" Reflecting On Purposes and Practice

We have not really budged a step until we take residence in someone else's point of view.

—John Erskine

Why does working in literacy and basic education evoke so many emotional reactions? While it is true that teaching is often an emotionally charged activity just by its very nature, when we adults find ourselves teaching other adults—older, younger, and of our own age—and teaching them the fundamentals of reading, writing, numeracy, and other related basic material that you and I probably learned as children, it can evoke some strong emotions. And these emotions can appear on both sides of the classroom. Without question, adult literacy education is one of the most emotionally laden fields of education that exists, both for the learners and us as practitioners, again suggesting that professionalism in literacy is the combined strength of knowledge, skills, and values.

AN OPENING ACTIVITY

It is not easy to suddenly step outside ourselves and start thinking about our values. This chapter will be more personally meaningful if you first complete the exercise below. So please open your learning journal and take a few minutes to put down your thoughts on the statements shown below.

SOME THINGS I BELIEVE

1) I believe that the most important purpose of adult literacy education is to _____

_____

_____

2) I believe that my purpose as an adult literacy educator is to

_____

_____

3) I believe my responsibility to my students is to _____

_____

_____

4) I believe it is the students' responsibility to _____

_____

_____

5) My thoughts on philosophy with respect to teaching are __

_____

_____

Some of the Rewards of Teaching Literacy

I can speak from experience on this. In my own case, I really had no ambitions to work with low-literate adults some 40 years ago. Like so many who "fall into this field," I entered it because I needed a job. I was newly married and was working on a master's thesis. I had never heard of adult education, but when offered a job, I thought I could probably teach literacy for a year and then move on. To my surprise, the students *taught me*. One of the graduates went on to small engine mechanics. When I met him years later, he was working in heavy construction in the High Arctic making far more in wages than I ever will. Another decided that he needed to deal with his drinking problems and enrolled in AA. On the last day of the program, the married couple in the class came forward and thanked me for saving their marriage. These life changes were but a few of the stories that changed my life.

Now, three decades later as a professor of adult education, consider this. I was asked to be part of getting the first literacy program on my campus to help the physical plant workers, security staff, and housekeeping staff improve their academic skills. They were being asked to take an employment training program but were having problems due to the lack of basic skills. The course was a great success. Then, not so long ago, one of the campus physical plant staff whom I had seen working around the campus grounds came to my office and said he wanted to shake my hand. Reaching out, he said, "Thank you." I asked why. He said, "I know you were involved in getting the literacy courses on campus. Just yesterday I was mopping the floor of the Music Building. I've done it a million times. But yesterday I looked up at a poster on the wall. And guess what? I could read it!" Today, he delivers the mail around the campus. He never could have before and has been promoted several times. He has since told me, "I have a brand new life."

A brand new life is what thousands realize every year across North America thanks to the efforts of adult literacy tutors, teachers, administrators, and funding agencies. My brand new life as a result of "falling into this field" is not an uncommon story either. According to Sabatini et al. (2002), of 423 ABE teachers surveyed in the United States, "most respondents said they entered the field not because they specifically had targeted adult basic education as a career but because a position was open" (Smith & Hofer, 2002, pp. 5–6). A still earlier study (Galbraith & Zelenak, 1989) found the same: "The typical practicing adult educator is new to the position, has little or no course work in adult education, comes from a field outside of adult education, . . . and works very hard."

Yet, for so many who come into teaching adult basic education—indeed fall into it—the passage of time does not reduce the impact and sense of reward that adult literacy has on most practitioners. Thirty years later, I continue to believe this is the most important work one can do in the entire field of education—and I'm far from alone in this.

WHY DO WE TEACH?

One of the points made in Chapter 1, and seen again in Chapter 2, was that each of us brings a set of perspectives and personal values to this work. Let's think about these perspectives for a minute. To begin, consider how you reacted to the various historical vignettes in the last chapter. Were there some you were very attracted to or impressed with? Were there others that may have impressed you but you then thought, "That's not for me. I couldn't do that." Some may have looked at the social justice work of Jane Addams and Moses Coady as being "too radical for me." But other literacy teachers believe the approach of such educators is the only meaningful way to bring about real change in the lives of our learners.

Similarly, some may have been uncomfortable with the expressed missionary agenda of William Smith and the Methodists of the early Bristol schools, and also perhaps with the version of evangelism seen among the Port Royalists. One participant I had in a workshop on the history of literacy thought "using the Bible to 'convert people'" was reprehensible. On the other hand, another practitioner who came to a workshop presentation on this same topic was so enthralled to see the legacy of the Bible being used in literacy that he said this affirmed his efforts, and he left committed to put all of his efforts into literacy as his life's work.

The reactions are as varied as the approaches to literacy. Let's consider why we teach. What it means to us, what it may mean to others, and if there are philosophical approaches we never considered before, but maybe should. Robert Blakely once told us: "We can—and usually do—refrain from asking philosophical questions, but we cannot avoid acting according to philosophical assumptions." (1957, p. 93). What are the options for how we approach our teaching? What other approaches and choices do we have? How do others see this field, and why? Why do we sometimes seem to have conflicts with others around purposes?

Here are the main "working philosophies" that are found in the mainstream adult education literature as adapted to our practice in literacy.

"TO BE EDUCATED": THE LIBERAL ADULT EDUCATION PHILOSOPHY

According to Elias and Merriam (2005), the liberal adult education perspective is the oldest and most enduring philosophy of education in the Western world. Its influence on what constitutes "an education" is immeasurable. Elsewhere (Quigley, 1997), I have discussed liberal education with the observation that it "rests on the premise that . . . education should be grounded in the cultural knowledge base of the Western world" (p. 117). This means education, from this approach, should be based on "literature, history, philosophy, political ideas, critical thinking, and self-knowledge" (117). Here is the knowledge of the dominant culture in our Western civilization. As Beder succinctly put it, the liberal approach to education focuses on "the cultivation of the intellect" (1989, p. 44). It is the basis of most liberal arts and sciences degrees and the vast amount of content that makes up the schooling curricula in industrialized nations.

Some criticize this approach, saying it is but "education for its own sake" with no real *practical* value. But scholars and thinkers dating to ancient Greece would argue it is as "practical" as wisdom itself. A liberal education dates at least to Plato's academy and Benjamin Franklin's Juntos (Grattan, 1955, 1959), where classic books were read and discussed, to the Great Books program, and more recently to the defense of the liberal arts by E. D. Hirsch in his book: *Cultural literacy: What every American needs to know* (1988). Thomas Jefferson stressed the need for an educated citizenry in his *Preamble to the Bill for the More General Diffusion of Knowledge*, insisting on a liberal education for all Americans: "Those whom nature hath endowed with genius and virtue should be rendered by a liberal education worthy to receive, and able to guard the sacred deposit for the rights and liberties of their fellow citizens" (cited in Elias & Merriam, 2005, pp. 22–23).

While the appropriate content for the arts has been the source of endless debate through time, it typically has a prescribed canon of knowledge. As seen in Chapter Two, the designated education for the illiterate of the 19th century was the Bible, and the Bristol School taught this alone. The Scriptures made up some of the content for the Freedmen of Port Royal. In both, the curriculum was *decided for* learners and this was the starting point for Hull House as well, even if goals changed later.

The liberal perspective is highly active in adult literacy today and often effectively defines our very field. Today, reading and writing ability is measured and total numbers of low-literate adults are determined in national studies such as the 1993 *National Adult Literacy Study* (e.g., Kirsch, Jungeblut, Jenkins, & Kolstad), and the 2000 and 2005 *International Adult Literacy Surveys* (OECD, 2000). How does the measuring take place? Using measures in the dominant language of the culture in now 40 countries, the International Adult Literacy Surveys uses reading, writing, and numeracy content chosen to be representative of everyday usage. With face-to-face interviews with adults with low literacy skills, we get national and international reports on the state of adult literacy. This is the liberal approach to literacy in the sense that these reports are not based on "students' critical thinking ability" or on "the fulfillment of learner-identified needs" or their "capacity to get and hold jobs." The criteria for North American levels of adult literacy are effectively determined on criteria for what it means "to be educated." Thomas Jefferson's view of what it means "to be educated," according to an external set of judgments on cultural content, prevails in so much of literacy today that it is remarkable.

As suggested in Chapter 2, the liberal tradition in adult literacy has been shaped and re-shaped countless times by social, institutional, governmental, and religious institutions. As a result, we have had centuries of moralizing, politicizing, rhetoric, and endless disagreements in adult literacy around what constitutes an "appropriate curriculum," what makes up "appropriate knowledge," and what "a proper education" means.

I can think of many ABE and basic literacy teachers who have fervently taken this approach in their classrooms. One teacher who comes to mind was very committed to the liberal tradition. I was teaching social and vocational skills at a community college, and she taught the English classes. I remember how insistent she was that her students needed to read Shakespeare. Her reasoning went this way: "My students have to go out into the world and, to succeed, they need to be at least 'somewhat educated.' They need at least some familiarity with good literature. At least to the extent of knowing who Shakespeare and other classic writers were, how they wrote, and what some of the Great Books are about. Why teach English otherwise?"

Grammar, spelling, and writing skills came first, but her basic education students were introduced to *Macbeth*, *Pride and Prejudice*, and several other of the classics of literature as soon as possible in her curriculum. Her firm belief was "to deny students some basic knowledge of literature was to do them a disservice. To let them leave without a true education."

Do you disagree? If so, how would you have argued with her? On what grounds?

THE LIBERAL EDUCATION PHILOSOPHY IN YOUR CLASSROOM

The liberal education tradition is a longstanding, highly respected approach to literacy and education. It provides a window to the dominant culture of our society. But how can it be applied to adult literacy?

For purposes of skill development and "practicality" in education, this approach has given rise to considerable work on critical thinking and critical reading skills (i.e., Brookfield, 1988,

1995). The use of stories, novels, poetry, plays, and film in the liberal tradition can have an important role in literacy teaching and learning. A type of therapy has been developed for children, especially, in the psychology of reading referred to as bibliotherapy (i.e., Ouzts, 1991; Riordan & Wilson, 1989). The use of bibliotherapy has been used with adults in prison literacy as well.

I had a graduate student explore the use of video tapes on issues like domestic violence and sexual abuse with the incarcerated men she worked with in prison literacy. The videos gave a safe distance from the issues for the inmates. The discussion among the men that followed often lead to their seeing their lives in very different ways. One said he always thought being a man meant being "tough," but now he could see how that view hurt others (Gillette, 1998).

It can develop critical thinking skills and bring learners to think about situations and issues relevant to their lives. Indeed, some say we shouldn't link education with literacy if we are not engaged in the "education" understood by the very label we apply to our own work.

However, one of the major criticisms of the liberal tradition has been that the so-called "canon of worthy knowledge" is decided by others irrespective of learners' needs or the expressed interests of the community. Decisions on content typically privilege one culture and one history. And in North America at least, we frequently end up with the dominant white culture deciding what constitutes "the most important knowledge" for all. There are, of course many exceptions. In this, many today argue that liberal studies of the cultures and histories of minorities is essential for all to be educated, while others point out that the liberal tradition can help adults become "bi-cultural and bi-lingual" if the liberal curriculum brings together knowledge and appreciation of more than one culture.

But despite the singularity of mind that my teacher friend displayed as she introduced Shakespeare to her ABE class, the liberal philosophy is not the *only* approach, nor does it have to be the *exclusive approach* and the "one and only way" in literacy.

"COME ON, LET'S FIND OUT": THE PROGRESSIVE ADULT EDUCATION PHILOSOPHY

Thinking of the difference between a liberal education and a progressive education might be compared with a jigsaw puzzle exercise. You are given a puzzle with a picture on the box top. You study the picture, and then you begin to fit the pieces together. Another approach is to not look at the cover at all. Just set the pieces on the table and go about "discovering your way." The two approaches are very different, and the difference is important to teaching philosophies. Some teachers enter the classroom and put the "five points we will learn about today" on the whiteboard, and then discuss what the students read or worked on yesterday with the given outline in front of everyone. In other words, the picture is presented, and it is for the students to follow along and see how the pieces fit in. Another teacher enters the room and says: "Here are five problems. I'm going to write them on the board. Let's then go into groups and see what we come up with for answers. Then, let's draw up a list of what we learned today from this on the whiteboard by the end of today's class."

The school of philosophical thought called "progressive education" (Elias & Merriam, 2005; Merriam & Brockett, 1997) comes from an important tradition in American educational history. As we enter the classroom or the tutoring situation, we have to first ask if we should teach with "the cover on or the cover off." For progressive educators, we are not teaching content alone but *how to think in pragmatic, useful ways* within content areas that can serve the learner in and outside the classroom. By some accounts, here is the very essence of what American education is all about. As the literature on the history and culture of America supports (i.e., Cremin, 1964; Button & Provenzo, 1983), the progressive approach to learning has deep roots in America. From the very outset, the American Dream has carried the belief that people have the freedom and the capacity to form their own destiny. They can and should learn from the past, of course—as the liberal approach advocates—

but the skills we bring to the present moment are the essentials for solving the challenges of tomorrow. We can learn by doing, as Kurt Lewin said, and it is this that will build a society. Pragmatics are far better than any history or literary discourse in this philosophy.

The issue here is the major role of "agency" in North American culture. Every individual has the free will and the right to act on that free will in a democracy. Lived-experience matters, problem-solving skills matter, common sense and clear reasoning matter. Few have expressed this better than William James, who taught at Harvard in the late 1800s. According to Ralph Barton Perry, James's work is "the most perfect philosophical expression of American individualism" (cited in Cremin, 1964, p. 108). For James, "voluntarism, not determinism, is the crucial fact of human affairs" (p. 106). Intellectual leaders such as Rousseau, Pestalozzi, Froebel, and in America, Charles Pierce and John Dewey infused this perspective into the system of school education believing this was the foundation for democracy. Dewey believed "education would flourish if it took place in a democracy; democracy would develop if there was true education" (Elias & Merriam, 2005, p. 55). Because experience and problem solving are so central to this philosophy, Dewey later increased his emphasis on the value of experimentalism and the fundamentals methods of science. As he saw it, "individuals achieve freedom as they master the tools of learning that are available" (Elias & Merriam, p. 56).

Little has changed in mainstream adult education in this respect. Compare what historian Harold Stubblefield recently envisioned mainstream adult education should be doing into the future. In an article published in 2002, he said our field should be engaged in "*identifying and framing solutions to problems* [italics added] at the community level in collaboration with other interested individuals and groups" (p. 5). He suggests both professors and practitioners of adult education should "participate in collaborative action research projects . . . beyond the routine functions of their job and institutional setting" (p. 6), thereby contributing to and becoming exposed to "the broader field of adult education" (p. 6). Action research is the topic of the final chapter in this series, but it naturally arises from this progressive education approach.

If the philosophy of progressive education is based on inductive thinking—"teaching with the cover off"—then the Antigonish Movement, which most would place in the radical category, can also be argued as being in the progressive tradition. Here was a massive problem-solving "project" with only the issues, some guidance, and lots of encouragement as guidelines. The Hull House experience was the same. As the movement matured, problems were posed, problems were addressed, and some were solved on a grand scale.

THE PROGRESSIVE PHILOSOPHY IN YOUR CLASSROOM

Looking now at adult literacy more specifically, in the progressive tradition there needs to be a teaching shift from "educating" to "learning." The teacher stimulates, organizes, "instigates," sets up situations, introduces challenges, and evaluates in an environment of discovery. The possibility of teacher and learner discovering and learning together is very real here. Paul Jurmo (1989) is one who has argued for a participatory approach to literacy and ABE. Compare this statement by Jurmo to those we saw in the liberal approach: "The teacher does not rely on one universally applicable instructional method. Instead, the teacher *should seek to set up a learning environment* [italics added] that encourages the learner to explore a variety of forms of written language and find the ones that are particularly meaningful" (p. 19).

As in the liberal philosophy, an important question that arises here is: "Who decides?" For the liberal approach, most of what is taught and learned is decided based on an agreed upon canon that "should" be covered. In the progressive philosophy, decision making is often (not always) shared between the teacher and learner, or learner and learner.

The progressive approach to literacy is time honored and very natural in the sense that problem posing and problem solving are what all adults do during most of our waking hours. Also, it takes a level of pressure off the teacher to "perform," in that students are expected to be part of many decisions, to be part of the choices made within the environment the teacher and learners seek to create. It can bring a class together around a common set of problems or the problems of one or more students. And, since it is about discovery and inductive exploration, it can be stimulating and fun for the teacher as well.

I once had a graduate student who taught the state's DUI program as required for those who had been arrested for driving under the influence of alcohol. His curriculum was not only required teaching, but his method was to be strictly lecture-and-test. His students were there by requirement of the courts. Teaching had to consist of "hard facts," measurable knowledge. No room for "learner input" or fun here. But he explained in our graduate class that his job was growing deathly boring, and he was sure his court-ordered students were not learning much more than what was required on the exam. Although it put his very job at risk, he decided to divide a new group of adults into two groups. One he lectured to in the usual way; one went into another room with a set of questions and print materials on drinking and driving. When he tested the two groups, those who had worked together did better. And they did so every time, group after group.

However, one of the first criticisms of the progressive approach is that *it is time consuming*. The teacher's biggest enemy every day is time. The time it will take "to discover" can never be predicted with accuracy. Further, there is no absolute guarantee that the learners will discover "what they are supposed to," or that they will learn and take away "what they are supposed to." Moreover, since the progressive approach can deviate from the curriculum, it can require a lot of confidence on the part of the teacher to make it successful.

Problem-solving may not be what you have tried in your classroom or tutoring work, and it may not be what you are comfortable with initially, but there is no question that it is worth considering, since ownership of learning, the challenge of problem solving, and finding collaborative ways to achieve relevance are all very powerful methods in adult education. Many adult learners have said they want to be challenged and stimulated (Quigley, 1997), not to have basic education made "boring" like their past schooling experiences. This is one way to do that.

However, neither does this have to be the "one best way." There are yet other approaches. Let's look at the one that has dominated so much of our field in recent years.

"GETTING STUDENTS JOB-READY": THE VOCATIONAL ADULT EDUCATION PHILOSOPHY

Most conversations at literacy conferences and meetings are not about history and philosophy; they are usually about funding—or more exactly, about lack for funding. How our programs get funded, what the new program thrusts are (if any), and what direction funding agencies may want us to go in—these issues virtually take on a life of their own. And little wonder. In 1990, Forest Chisman estimated that, to eliminate illiteracy in the U.S. for those without any basic skills and, secondly, reach what he calls "threshold skills" for the others with some literacy problems, including ESL, "by the demographic deadline of 2010" (p. 254), would cost "about $12 billion per year" (p. 254).

Interestingly, Chisman made the case that such funding should come from four sources: "the federal government, employers, states, and localities" (1990, p. 255). For Chisman, here are the four "obvious funders" of adult literacy. Not faith-based organizations and churches, as in Bristol, Port Royal, or the Antigonish Movement. Not through collaboration with philanthropic organizations or families, like Hull House. Government at various levels and employers are typically assumed to be the appropriate sponsors of literacy because almost every major governmental policy on literacy since World War II has placed the onus on some level of government sponsorship for funding. However, behind such funding usually lies the further assumption that the primary reasons to justify this public spending is the "payback." It will help the economy and build the work-force. Consistent with much of our literacy history, the issue is not what learners need but what society needs at any given moment. And the workforce has been the perceived dominant need for North America for decades.

As seen in the previous chapter, in the early 19th century the social imperative for adult literacy was morality. At the turn of the 20th century, we saw programs concerned with democracy and social justice. But following World War II, with the advent of "manpower planning" and human capital formation for economic gain, federal governments in many industrialized nations worked to bring about increased productivity by social engineering programs such as literacy, and what was later called "adult basic education" (Quigley, 1997).

For most adult education teachers, this translates into assisting learners to be able to perform well in the work world. Vocational in purpose, this approach is typically behaviorist in nature (Elias & Merriam, 2005). By building the types of job skills employers will want, we can take some pride in the knowledge that we had a hand in helping a student walk into an employment position and say with new confidence: "I can do this job." There is dignity in work and pride in mastering the skills that make work more accessible. Many of our learners come to our programs looking to receive a GED diploma, ABE diploma, or ESL certificate. Why? In my experience and in most of the research, many hope the knowledge gained from a literacy program will help them improve their lives in some very specific way. Even if it is not as singularly important to every learner as some legislation would want, improved employment options are often among the ways they hope their lives will improve.

There is nothing really new in this. As seen in models like the Antigonish Movement, Frontier College, and Hull House, it can be part of individual, community, and regional change. While there are different approaches to vocational literacy and complex political and ethical issues around vocational literacy, the fundamental philosophical approach will typically be a behavioral one. As Elias and Merriam state: "Probably no other system . . . has had as much impact on general and adult education [as behaviorism]" (2005, p. 83).

Yet just as Chisman assumed that government and the corporate sector should be the "normal funders" of literacy, practitioners can find themselves teaching to the sponsor's goals more than the learners'. This has become "normalized" in many instances. There are ABE administrators who dare not write a grant proposal from any perspective other than purely vocational—even if the teaching will meet a greater range of learner needs if the grant is received. A purely liberal or, for that matter, purely progressive philosophy will rarely meet governmental "job-sponsorship" requirements. As a result, some teachers will start their teaching with a concern for self-esteem, some with a concern for problem-solving skills, some with the deficit of knowledge they perceive in their learners, but it is typically the administrator who has to figure out, "What do we do faced with the demands of funders, and what do we put in the final report to the funding agencies?" The ethical issues in literacy around this working philosophy, and throughout this field, are real.

However one chooses to react to these, it is obvious that philosophy—and conflicts over philosophy—are inescapable in this field of ours. To discuss professionalism without reflection on the ethics and efficacies of working philosophies is to miss a huge part of what we do (Argyris, 1989; Schön, 1983).

In reflecting on vocationalism and the behavioral philosophy behind it, it can be seen that it has a lot in common with the liberal approach. The curriculum content is typically decided externally—that is, decided with a good deal of consideration for what the "profession," the employer, or the "job market" may deem as necessary rather than the learner. The content is not the canon of literary and cultural knowledge that the liberal approach will expect, but vocationalism typically draws from criteria *outside* the program and measures itself by standards set outside the classroom. But unique to this philosophical approach is its underpinning of behaviorism. Typically, observable behaviors, observable values, and observable as well as measurable performance levels must be seen and must be able to be determined in quantifiable ways to have credible vocationalism.

In fact, vocationalism can go in at least two directions. In "functional" vocational literacy, the curriculum is set *for* learners—rarely by them or with them—and is measured according to criteria set by employers and experts knowledgeable about the work force (Gowen, 1992). This approach once took the form of competency-based education for adult literacy during the 1970s and 1980s (Quigley, 1997). Harkening to the functionalist approach to education and professionalism seen in Chapter One, under competency-based literacy, the required competencies for literacy were set and measured by external experts. As Gowen states it: "[The] functional context not only assumes certain characteristics about knowledge, it also supports specific assessment measures. What constitutes a literacy skill and how that skill is measured are both directly tied to quantifiable measures of specific tasks" (pp. 16–17).

However, the competency-based movement for literacy in America collapsed in the late 1970s. One critique was that it typically ignored critical thinking, problem solving, or the development of what some would consider team or leadership skills (Collins, 1983). Moreover, in the 1960s and 1970s, the Competency Based Adult Education (CBAE) movement ignored issues of motivation and life issues—what may be called the "affective domain." Competency-based education didn't particularly concern itself with issues that arise in families, in neighborhoods, or in life itself. Self-efficacy, self-confidence, or group skills were rarely mentioned. It also assumed the workplace was a fair and supportive place. The single concern in the competency-based movement was how to prepare the learner to do the job with measurable competencies, not with what to do on the job if racism or sexism or discrimination arose, how to address problems in the workplace or in life, or how to participate in society with a liberal education.

Vocational is the only approach in some situations for some learners. And it appeals more to some teachers, administrators, and sponsors than others to the point that it is sometimes seen as the one-best-way for all situations and learners by some policy makers and educators. Still, there are variations on vocational theme. As Gowen explains, the "worker-centered approach" (1992, p. 15) is where problem-solving skills, troubleshooting abilities, critical thinking, anticipation of problems, and a wider overview and concern for the work and the workplace can be fostered. In this variation of the vocational model, tasks to be learned and performed are largely decided by and with the student. In this sense, the vocational model effectively borrows some of the progressive philosophy.

Worker-centered vocational literacy begins by assuming *what is learned*, *how it is learned*, and *how the learning is measured* are not entirely the domain of the teacher, tutor, mentor, or instructor. Content and process are open for negotiation. But behaviorism is nevertheless the essence of all vocationalism since the ultimate test comes from performance, and it will ultimately be decided in the workplace who is "best trained." The issues and decisions that arise for programs and practitioners in this approach to literacy often are not sufficiently discussed in programs, with policy makers, with employers, or even with the learners.

THE VOCATIONAL PHILOSOPHY IN YOUR CLASSROOM

Behaviorism is what most of us know best. From B. F. Skinner to Ralph Tyler (Merriam & Brockett, 1997), the behaviorist approach has been the touchstone of public schooling curricula throughout much of the 20th century. Meeting measurable standards and being able to perform certain skills are what most of us saw in school. The frequent "back-to-basics" drives in schools are typically a call for a return to more measurable skills and knowledge. And, it needs to be noted, behaviorism in a schooling model is what many of our adult learners *expect to see* when they come back, since past schooling is typically their one point of reference. How to combine elements of vocationalism with the other philosophies—including your own philosophy—is seen in the next chapter.

"THE LEARNER COMES FIRST":
THE HUMANIST ADULT
EDUCATION PHILOSOPHY

This is the philosophy that most practitioners in our field intuitively follow, even if they are not always aware of it. Humanism has deep roots in education and in Western civilization—roots that arise from the firm belief that every human being is guided by reason, by intuition, and by emotion. The humanist philosophy says that human nature is essentially good, curiosity comes from within and is an innate quality, and students do not need to be "motivated" because we are all born naturally motivated—some simply become "de-motivated" along the way. The challenge is to rekindle that fire. In many ways, humanism sets the highest level *for student-centered* teaching of any the philosophies.

Adult educator Malcolm Knowles is credited with popularizing and refining the humanist philosophy for teaching adults in mainstream adult education. When asked: "How do you define an adult?" (Knowles, 1980), he did not go to work issues or problem solving. He said: "A person is an adult to the extent that that individual perceives herself or himself to be essentially responsible for her or his own life" (p. 24). Self-perception, internal motivation, self-fulfillment, personal goals—these are all championed in Knowles's humanistic understanding of who adults are.

For Knowles, our job as adult educators is to "help individuals to develop the attitude that learning is a lifelong process and to acquire the skills of self-directed learning" (p. 28). He emphasizes "attitude," not knowledge or skills. He says "help," not "teach." The goal for Knowles is not necessarily to ensure adults pass exams, get jobs, or become more critical; these are teacher-based and funder-based agendas along the line of the many historical models we saw in Chapter One. In fact none of the historical landmarks, with the possible exception of the Antigonish Movement, actually set out to help learners realize their own dreams and ambitions through literacy based on the goals that *they* had. Humanism is a late 20th century addition to literacy education.

Knowles's main methodological contribution to theory and practice is what he termed and popularized as *andragogy* (e.g., Knowles, 1980). This is important because, for Knowles, the ways children are taught—what he calls *pedagogy*—were traditionally "top-down" approaches. He argued that adults are not the same as children, and they should not be taught as children using a pedagogical approach. He puts the adult learner at the center of teaching, using the term *andra*, or adult (or man) from the Greek, together with *gogy*, meaning to teach. This he contrasted with *pedagogy*, which he took to mean the teaching of children from *peda*, meaning child, together with *gogy* (1980). "The art and science of helping adults learn" (1980, p. 43), as he described it, has made a huge impact on mainstream adult education, since it means the learner is legitimately at the very core of adult teaching.

Since so many teachers and tutors intuitively turn to this approach in their classrooms, Knowles's work should be of greater interest in adult literacy. For instance, Knowles was very interested in using learning contracts with learners. In this approach, the learner develops and conducts a learning endeavor as agreed upon with the facilitator (Knowles, 1975). The use of learning contracts where adult learners choose the content and process, even the evaluation methods, in negotiation with the facilitator are remarkably rare in a field that often describes itself as learner-centered and "humanist."

In our field, Hanna Fingeret and Paul Jurmo have strengthened the humanist approach through the literature by taking the position that we need to work to share decision making with our learners through *participatory literacy* (i.e., Fingeret & Jurmo, 1989). They do not say learners decide everything that is done in the classroom, or ignore the program curriculum or the end-testing. In participatory learning, content, methods and evaluation are negotiated with the learners.

Fingeret (1983) was one of the researchers in recent years who challenged researchers and practitioners to be more critical about what they may be seeing. She problematized many of the assumptions we carry. As she explains it, researchers and practitioners may *think* they are observing adult learners who have little self-esteem, but learners are being observed in a "schooling context." They may well be "made to feel powerless" (Fingeret, 1989, p. 10) in such a setting. They may be experiencing the re-occurring, disempowering schooling experience that caused them to quit school in the first place (Quigley, 1997). She argues that it may be a mistake to conclude that adults with low literacy skills *always* have low self-esteem. Researchers and practitioners alike might consider visiting their adult learners in the own communities where they actually live and work, as Fingeret did. Seeing adults with low literacy skills in their own context, she found them self-assured living in what she calls "rich social networks" (Fingeret, 1983). She found communities where people help one another, share the resources they have, and act with all the self-esteem that any mother, father, spouse, or partner may display. Literacy or no literacy.

However, while Fingeret's is a legitimate point of view, the critique of andragogy, or participatory methods in literacy for that matter, is that there is a risk of "romanticizing" adults with low literacy skills (Quigley, 1987). Fingeret once pointed out that "simply working with a caring individual is not enough" (Fingeret & Danin, 1991, p. 10). Fingeret and Jurmo have presented participatory literacy as giving learners active roles in the "control, responsibility, and reward" (1989, p. 18) of all program activities and would agree with Knowles that developing self-directed learners is a major goal for humanist adult education. Caring teachers who subscribe to humanism need to be caring enough to build upon the self-reliance that their adult learners bring to programs. Inter-dependence is one way, as suggested in the next chapter.

Having a clear working philosophy and acting on it, being aware of other philosophical options, being open to revising one's own approach, understanding why others may do what they do while knowing when to adopt aspects of other philosophies when this makes sense—these are not easy. In fact, professionalism is not easy. But when we see the results, it helps put things back into perspective and builds our sense of pride in our work.

THE HUMANIST PHILOSOPHY IN
YOUR CLASSROOM

In humanism, the learners and the learners' needs are central to teaching and learning (Rogers, 1983). The learners' reservoir of knowledge is necessary for the educational process to succeed, and learners are encouraged to take some levels of ownership of their program. Yet as Jurmo (1989) explains: "Traditionally, literacy students have been handed a prescribed set of topics, materials, and activities that they are expected to master. Learner-centered programs give learners some control in the planning of instructional activities" (Jurmo, 1989, p. 29; Fingeret & Danin, 1991). More examples of this are seen in the next chapter, but Jurmo tells us that teachers can have learners respond to open-ended questions on content, build learning materials and processes from their own life experiences, and encourage feedback for evaluation which is then discussed and acted upon by the entire class. Peer teaching, writing journals or newsletters, undertaking written activities with group meetings, and discussions can be part of the participatory learning process. Field trips, artistic activities, role playing, team research projects, and other participatory activities can raise involvement and be part of participatory decision making.

As noted earlier, Knowles advocates that learners can learn as individuals and in groups around projects or topics that they conduct on the basis of a "learning contract" with the teacher. Jurmo goes further with this discussing how learners can be involved in fund-raising, act on various learner boards, and be part of recruiting drives. In Canada, authors such as Pat Campbell (2001) give research and suggestions for use of student journals and personal narratives in the classroom. Mary Norton (2001) has written on the successes of peer tutoring and participatory education in her program in Edmonton, Alberta, Canada. Jenny Horsman, in her book *Too scared to learn: Women, vio-*

lence and education (1999), has written on women's learning
and women who are facing violent situations in their lives.
Howard Davidson (2001) has written about participatory practices in prison literacy education, and Mary Ellen Belfiore and
Sue Folinsbee (2000) have discussed ways to make good use of
participatory literacy in the workplace.

In each of these settings, humanistic literacy seeks to put
more decision making in the hands of the learner based on the
learner's expressed needs. In answer to the perennial questions:
"Who makes the decisions, based on what criteria, and what
process for decision making is being used?" the humanist's answer will always involve the learner.

"LIBERATE, DON'T 'DOMESTICATE' ": THE RADICAL ADULT EDUCATION PHILOSOPHY

Paolo Freire's maxim that all education either liberates or
domesticates would place all the above philosophies into the
"domesticating" category. What is sometimes called the "libera-
tory" or the "critical" philosophy (Merriam & Brockett, 1997)
or even the countercritique (Beder, 1989) has long been referred
to as the "radical philosophy" in adult education (Elias & Merriam, 2005). The term "radical" is appropriate if we consider
its early roots. The *Shorter Oxford Dictionary* tells us that in
1562 the word "radical" referred to "going to the root or origin;
esp. change or cure" (Little, et al., 1970, p. 1648). As a change
for individual and social oppression, the radical tradition also
has a very long history in adult education and in our literacy
field in particular.

Perhaps the most famous adult educator in this tradition,
if not in all of adult education, is Paulo Freire(1973). His work
in literacy with the poor and peasant workers in Brazil and later
in Chile involved teaching adults to "name their world" as they
learned to read and write. This meant adult learners became increasingly conscious of their world and how it was socially constructed. They came to see the world differently. Not unlike the

world we live in, Freire saw people being made "susceptible to populist manipulation by power elites, by force, propaganda, slogans, or dehumanizing utilization of technology" (Elias & Merriam, 2005, p. 157). However, through *conscientization*, there can occur "a radical denunciation of dehumanizing structures, accompanied by an announcement of a new reality to be created" (p. 157). Literacy learners can achieve what we might think of as critical consciousness. In Freire's approach, learners can gain a new critical consciousness of the political, economic, and social oppression they are living under. How?

In Brazil and Chile, when the peasant workers learned to read and write, they used what was essentially a problem posing/problem solving approach with dialog and discussion. The literacy programs began "with an investigation of the cultural situation of the learners" (Elias & Merriam, 2005, p. 159). As they learned to read and write, they learned and talked about the poverty, living conditions, working conditions, and power imbalances in their world. They began to ask if their "station in life" was truly "God-given," or "normal" or "fair." Seeing the world through new, more critical eyes, thousands of peasants in Latin America were moved to question the power structures that controlled their lives.

Freire never advocated revolution and disagreed with his contemporary, Che Guevera, noting that Guevera began and ended his concept of a revolution with mistrust, saying: "Do not trust your own shadow, never trust friendly peasants, informers, guides, or contact men..until the zone is liberated" (cited in Elias & Merriam, 2005, p. 161). Nevertheless Freire was banished from his home country of Brazil. After working in literacy education in Chile, and after years of teaching, writing, and traveling, including years teaching at Harvard University, he returned to Brazil and worked in the school system at the end of his life.

Clearly, individual liberation and societal liberation are closely connected in Freire's approach to literacy, and we have, in the radical philosophy, an approach to education unlike the others seen so far. As Beder (1989) puts it, "Unlike the liberal-progressive tradition, those associated with the countercritique [or radicalism as named here] consider capitalist democracy to be inherently flawed by structural inequalities that can be re-dressed only by substantially reordering of the social system" (p. 45). The focus of the radical philosophy is on systemic change with a more critical view of the society we live in, not on sin-gular individual change that can only lead to conformity within an unjust society. In the Antigonish Movement and Hull House, literacy was not the first, most pressing, issue. Poverty, inequality, oppression, and how to empower people so they could take more control of their lives were the immediate issues. Literacy was an important tool—but only a tool. As Beder explains it: "Once learners become conscious of the forces that control their lives, they become empowered, and empowerment leads to action" (p. 47).

One of the most famous examples of the radical philosophy at work is Highlander Folk School, located in New Market, Ten-nessee, and famous for its long history of radical adult education work (Bell, Gaventa, & Peters, 1990). One example of their work concerning literacy was when their adult education work-ers traveled to Johns Island, South Carolina, to help develop a Citizenship School. At the time, blacks on the island could not "read well enough to pass the voter registration requirement exam that was given by white registrars who were unsympa-thetic to blacks voting and used the restrictions of literacy as a means of keeping blacks from voting" (p. 68). Most of the resi-dents spoke Gullah, a mixture of English and African languages, along with some French (p. 68). Highlander helped the citizens teach literacy in English, and the citizens were able to vote and have a voice in their own political destiny.

The citizenship program they created caught the interest of Andrew Young and Martin Luther King. This became the chosen literacy program of the Southern Christian Leadership Conference as the civil rights movement grew. According to Myles Horton, then director of Highlander, "Andrew Young and other people think of it [the Sea Island story] as kind of basic to the civil rights movement . . . that program succeeded at a time that no other literacy programs were succeeding in the United States" (Bell, Gaventa, & Peters, 1990, p. 76). Like the Antigonish Movement, justice was the goal.

Some adult educators, including many literacy educators,

reject this approach, believing it can potentially lead to anarchy. Holding another philosophical analysis, they ask: "What if everyone were to attack 'the system'? Is this what our job consists of?" However, for those who work from this philosophy, this is the single approach that takes a wide, critical view of the cultural-economic-sociological context in which we live. Democracy means the "system should be attacked more often," they would say. Advocates of the radical philosophy criticize the other approaches as being too individualistic and psychologically oriented. Learners may leave "feeling good about themselves" and good about their new-found skills, but the world they re-enter will not have changed. What can they do but fall back into former patterns? From the radical viewpoint, to use Freire's terms, learners are being "domesticated," not "liberated" in most literacy programs. Most programs are raising false hopes and effectively perpetuating the oppressive systems and attitudes that Jane Addams and Moses Coady worked to change.

What should we be doing? From the radical perspective, we should be helping our learners become more aware of the inequities they, their families, and their communities are experiencing. We should help them become better informed of their personal rights and freedoms. They should leave programs knowing the democratic and legal avenues open to when they need them.

Today, the growing body of literature under the widening umbrella of adult education radicalism now includes such diverse cultural and sociological movements as feminist theory; Critical Theory; gay, lesbian and queer theory and activism; and critical worker education within union and peace movements (e.g., Cunningham, 1989; Merriam & Brockett, 1997). But looking back just for a minute, we saw the international efforts of Jane Addams and the women of Hull House, the regionwide work of Father Moses Coady and Father Jimmy Tompkins in the Maritime provinces, and had a glance at the Highlander experience in Johns Island. In these examples—and there are many others that could have been mentioned (Quigley, 1987)—we saw how adults were first helped to become conscious of the forces that control their lives, and then we saw adults becoming empowered. In every case, literacy led to societal structural change. But how can it actually be used in the classroom?

USING THE RADICAL PHILOSOPHY IN YOUR CLASSROOM

This approach to adult literacy education begins with the learners, as does humanism, but radicalism understands issues not as deriving from individuals' lives as much as from the systems and institutions that shape and affect lives.

Adult literacy practitioners and students have developed all types of programs and projects from the radical tradition. Students have taken their written grievances to city hall—sometimes armed with video cameras. Students have engaged in letter writing campaigns—sometimes to help gain funding and support for the very literacy program they are in. Learners have been on television, radio, and in newspapers, and spoken to countless organizations to discuss adult literacy issues and low support for programs. They have taken workplace issues to their employers and to corporate boards—sometimes through unions, sometimes through the courts. On-the-job grievances and complaints are commonly heard in the discussions held in many literacy programs. Some practitioners will turn those complaints into learning case studies on what an employee's rights are and what action one can take. The same with domestic violence and family abuse. In each case, action takes over where the discussions end so that change is far more likely into the future lives of learners.

The term "radical" has come to carry pejorative connotations, despite the root origins of the term. As you think about this philosophy, ask if this is really so "radical." Is it, perhaps, adults simply learning to address the problems they face in the society we live in more effectively? While this approach is not for everyone, is it for you? Would you be interested in trying it, or supporting someone who wants to?

Let's reflect on where we came from when we began this chapter. Let's think about some of the topics raised here around philosophical perspectives.

WHAT I BELIEVE:
SOME FURTHER REFLECTIONS

Please open your Learning Journal and revisit the statement shown below.

1) Thinking further about it, I now believe the purpose of adult literacy education is to _____ _____ _____

2) Based on the philosophies seen in this chapter, the one philo- sophical tradition that I think I adhere to most in my day-to- day practice is _____, followed close behind by the _____ _____ philosophy. I say this because _____ _____

3) One(s) that appeal to me, but I have never really tried, is(are) _____ I say this because _____ _____

4) I am thinking I might try to integrate one or more of these new philosophy(ies) into my work. The way I'm thinking of doing this is _____ _____

5) Looking back at my Beginning Reflections at the beginning of this chapter, I would now say I believe that my primary purpose as an adult literacy educator is to _____ _____ _____

6) Looking back, I would now say I believe my responsibility to students is to _____ _____

7) Looking back, I would now say it is the students' responsi- bility to _____ _____

CHAPTER 3 DISCUSSION TOPICS FOR CONSIDERATION IN YOUR LEARNING JOURNAL AND LEARNING CIRCLE

Having made two sets of entries in your learning journal from this chapter, now please get together with your co-learners and compare notes.

- How did the others complete the pre-post statements on philosophy?
- Were there any surprises? That is, did anyone find some unexpected changes in the statements after reading the chapter?
- What would you say the overall working philosophy *of your program* is? Why?
- Would you and your learning circle say there are any implicit or explicit differences in vision, policies, or practice between yourselves and your program(s)?
- How should these be addressed?
- If you or members of your learning circle want to try a different philosophical perspective, in part or in its entirety, how will you do this? And how can the group support them and learn from their efforts?
- What barriers are there to trying some new approaches? Can you or your group think of ways to address these barriers so that some experimentation can take place?

CHAPTER 3
ACTIVITY OPTIONS FOR FOLLOW-UP

1) Discuss these with your learners and see about trying a new approach, even for a short time, in the classroom. Keep notes in your journal on reactions and outcomes.

2) How about having the students give input to the process and the activities of a new approach? What if they took charge of the activity themselves? Keep notes on reactions and outcomes.

NOTE: If you want to try an action research activity to actually do a *systematic comparison* in areas like student retention numbers before and after trying a new philosophical approach, or look for measurable improvements in learner satisfaction within the program before and after, or test change in levels of learned content, or improve classroom participation levels—just as examples—you should go to Chapter 4 to help design such a project.

But to simply try some new ideas based on philosophical approach, go ahead. Report back to your co-learners what happened, though. And have fun with it.

The next chapter will help review some of the basic principles of teaching adults and some of the methods that have proven effective *within each of the philosophical approaches* seen in this chapter. But here are some reading suggestions to carry the ideas of this chapter further.

CHAPTER 3: FURTHER READING

Reflective Practice:

Schön, D. (1983). *The reflective practitioner: How professionals think in action.* New York: Basic Books.

Overviews of Adult Literacy Education Philosophy and Professionalism

Beder, H. (1989). Purposes and philosophies of adult education. In S. Merriam & P. Cunningham (Eds.), *Handbook of adult and continuing education* (pp. 37–50). San Francisco: Jossey-Bass.

Darkenwald, G., & Merriam, S. (1982). *Adult education: Foundations of practice.* New York: Harper & Row.

Elias, J., & Merriam, S. (2005). *Philosophical foundations of adult education.* Malabar, FL: Krieger.

Sabatini, J., Ginsberg, L., & Russell, M. (2002). Professionalization and certification for teachers. In J. Comings, B. Garner & C. Smith (Eds.), *Annual review of adult learning and literacy,* Vol. 3 (pp. 203–247). San Francisco: Jossey-Bass.

Smith, C., & Hofer, J. (2003). *The characteristics and concerns of adult basic education teachers* (NCSALL Report No. 26). Harvard University, Harvard Graduate School of Education, National Center for the Study of Adult Learning and Literacy.

The Liberal Philosophy:

Brookfield, S. (1988). *Developing critical thinkers.* San Francisco: Jossey-Bass.

Button, H., & Provenzo, E. (1983). *History of education and culture.* Englewood Cliffs, NJ: Prentice Hall.

The Progressive Philosophy:

Fingeret, A. (1983). Social network: A new perspective on independence and illiterate adults. *Adult Education Quarterly, 33*(3), 133–146.

Stubblefield, H. (2002). Forging a new mission: Implications from the experiences of antecedent national associations. *Adult Learning, 13*(4), 4–6.

The Vocational Philosophy:

Chisman, F. (1990). *Leadership for literacy: The agenda for the 1990s.* San Francisco: Jossey-Bass.

Collins, M. (1983). A critical analysis of competency-based systems in adult education. *Adult Education Quarterly, 3*(33), 174–182.

Gowen, S. (1992). *The politics of workplace literacy: A case study*. New York: Teachers College Press.

The Humanist Philosophy:

Campbell, P. & Burnaby, B. (Eds.), (2001). *Participatory practices in adult education.* Mahwah, NJ: Lawrence Erlbaum.

Davidson, H. (2001). Possibilities for participatory education through prisoners' own educational practices. In P. Campbell & B. Burnaby (Eds.), *Participatory practices in adult education* (pp. 237–264). Mahwah, NJ: Lawrence Erlbaum.

Fingeret, H., & Jurmo, p. (Eds.), (1989). *Participatory literacy education.* New Directions for Adult and Continuing Education No. 42. San Francisco: Jossey-Bass.

Knowles, M. (1980). *The modern practice of adult education.* New York: Cambridge University Press.

The Radical Philosophy:

Bell, B., Gaventa, J., & Peters, J. (1990). *We make the road by walking: Conversations on education and social change.* Philadelphia: Temple University Press.

Cunningham, P. (1989). Making a more significant impact in society. In A. Quigley (Ed.), *Fulfilling the promise of adult and continuing education* (pp. 33–46). New Directions for Continuing Education No. 44. San Francisco: Jossey-Bass.

Freire, P. (1973). *Pedagogy of the oppressed.* New York: Seabury Press.

Quigley, B. A., & Holsinger, E. (1993). Happy consciousness: Ideology and hidden curricula in literacy education. *Adult Education Quarterly, 44*(1), 17–33.

CHAPTER 4

"Bringing It All Together": Teaching and Learning in Daily Practice"

Many have written that instruction is a science. Some have argued it is an art. Others have said it is a craft or an intuitive skill. I am not completely sure. But I know this. When it is motivating, when there is a flow of learning and communication between instructor and learner, it is more than all have written or said it was. It is a dimension. Not something one practices or performs, but something one enters and lives.

—Raymond Wlodkowski

This chapter builds on what we have seen so far and gives some "hands-on" applications for classrooms and tutoring. First we will look at some of the challenges involved in teaching mainstream adults and some ways teaching adults differs from teaching children. Then, modifying these same principles, we will consider some of the unique challenges faced when we set out to teach adults with low literacy skills. Finally, to pull principles, practice, and your own practice philosophy together, a proposed interdependent approach to adult literacy and basic education follows. Although literacy programs are as varied as those who teach and tutor, this approach is nevertheless offered as a way to implement some of the principles seen so far and a way to help incorporate your philosophy. But it can also give you and your program a way to "test" what you will have read and discussed because this proposed model takes into consideration one of the most pressing challenges we have in literacy, namely, the issue of student dropout.

By trying the interdependent approach, you can ask: "Is the dropout rate in my class or program actually declining using this approach?" You can ask: "Is student satisfaction increasing?" Or related to your own mental health: "Am I enjoying this work more?" On a cursory level at least, you can judge whether you are finding an enhanced atmosphere of collaborative and increased interdependent learning. The next chapter will give some methods and techniques to test this more thoroughly with action research, and it will provide you with ways to test other ideas you may have had to that point as well. But let's now begin by considering some of the challenges when setting out to teach adults. How does teaching adult differs from teaching children? Is it the same?

HOW DOES TEACHING ADULTS DIFFER FROM TEACHING CHILDREN?

Have you ever found yourself saying: "I sound exactly like my mother!" Or, "I can't believe it. I'm turning into my father!" It's natural to turn back to what we know best when we are trying to set an example. It's also remarkably common to teach as we were taught. Not surprisingly, many adults who come to us will inadvertently assume something of a pupil-like, or child-like, dependency role at the outset of an adult education program. They reach back to their roles in school and, like us, they know schooling well. The role of child learner comes easily to so many of our adult learners since the effects of childhood schooling are life-long for us all. But the thing is, we are not teaching children. This is not "school," it's adult education.

If we are to be as effective as possible in our teaching and tutoring, the literature makes it very clear that there are important differences between the ways children and adults learn—and prefer to learn. This matters for teaching and tutoring adults. Let's take a look.

Treating Adults as Adults

Looking first at the sociological, or we can call it the "political level," it is important to remember that adults, not children, can directly affect social structures (Rubenson, 1989). It is adults who vote, adults who comprise the workforce, adults who make peace and war, and adults who make the decisions in families, communities, and society. When we look at our learners, we need to remember that they have social, political, family, and other culture-based and legal responsibilities. Such responsibilities are inescapable for all adults. Therefore, from a sociological point of view, it is the "context and structure" of the lives of our adult learners that are critical. How they live in the world and how they relate to it should define this field of ours and should inform how we view our learners. How we think of our learners and what we should reasonably expect from them need to be based on adult criteria.

If we treat adults as children, chances are they will respond in kind. But herein lies one of the first problems leading to dropping out. As will be seen, adults need to be treated as adults but, at the same time, many of our learners need high levels of consideration and support. These are not mutually exclusive. Although adults, not children, run the world, our learners may not always appear to be as "adult" as we might like, but we have to hold them to that standard irrespective of their age or maturity levels. We should reasonably expect that adult learners have adult responsibilities and will be assuming more adult responsibilities in the future. Treating adults as adults is critical if they are to respond as adults. This principle becomes especially important when young adults are in our classrooms; direct suggestions are given on this in a moment.

Age Matters

Besides the increasing responsibilities that adults either embrace or have thrust upon them, physical and physiological differences also occur as we mature. There are major teaching-learning implications in this. Researcher and writer Huey Long has acknowledged that "physiologically, psychologically, and sociologically adults are more diverse than children" (1990, p. 25). There is also research that focuses on physiological and psychological differences between adults and children (Merriam & Caffarella, 2005) and research on how the aging process takes its toll on our hearing ability, vision, energy levels. Likewise, our levels of health and how these factors should inform teaching are important in adult teaching. It is ironic, actually, how aging can be so obvious to us as adults—how much we think and talk about it for ourselves—yet how often it can get ignored in adult teaching. Here are a few points that arise from the literature on the physiology of aging and the implications of it for teaching and learning.

"Excuse me. I can't hear you." On hearing loss, Long has noted that older adults often express "greater concern about the effects of reduced hearing ability than . . . about problems with vision" (1983, p. 29; also see Knox, 1977). In fact, "most adults in the decade of their 30s begin to experience some hearing loss, mainly of higher tones" (Long, 1983, p. 72). "By age 65 . . . roughly a fourth of adults have some significant hearing impartment" (Bee, 2000, p. 72). The reason, evidently, is a gradual degeneration of the auditory nerves and "wear and tear" on the inner ear. Interestingly, research also tells us Long's observation that adults seem to show greater concern for hearing loss than vision may not be far wrong: "The rate of serious impairment is higher for hearing loss than for visual loss" (Bee, 1992, p. 104).

Teachers of adults need to be aware of hearing concerns and appreciate that many adult learners will not reveal a hearing problem in the classroom. Teachers typically have to "give permission" for adult learners to speak up in a group or be willing to speak privately to the teacher about a hearing problem. Just as we may find ourselves turning the television volume up as we get older, we need to be conscious of the clarity and volume of speaking levels, including videos or films, and ask frequently if everyone can hear well. Meanwhile, adult learners need to feel they can change their seating, move closer to the speaker, or simply ask others to speak more loudly or clearly.

"Excuse me. I'm having trouble seeing that." A huge percentage of the North American adult population wears glasses or contact lenses, but those approaching or over age 40 may also "be involved in the bifocal battle," as Long puts it (1983, p. 29). We are told that major changes occur in the eye "sometime in one's 30s, although most of us do not experience the effects of those changes until somewhat later" (Bee, 1992, p. 103). The lens of our eyes naturally thickens from childhood, but vision acuity and clarity declines and varies with the degree of thickening through adulthood. Besides this thickening on the lens, our eyes also begin to lose their accommodative power in our 30s, meaning they lose elasticity and adjust more slowly to light and darkness. It is not uncommon, for instance, for adults in their 40s or early 50s to experience discomfort with the oncoming glare of headlights while driving at night. Our eyes don't accommodate the rapid change needed. Our distance and depth perception also becomes less responsive, so the bifocal battle begins. Is vision loss inevitable? Almost. According to research from the U.S. Bureau of the Census, "over 95 percent of adults over 65 require glasses at least some time" (cited in Bee, 1992, p. 103).

Vision loss becomes particularly important in teaching adults with lower literacy skills because many will not be able to afford bifocals, contacts or prescription glasses; in fact, many will not be aware that they are having vision problems. But the signs will be there if we are sensitive to them. Having students move closer to the blackboard or change their seating, increasing the intensity of the lighting in the room, or just letting the learners know they can ask for help in reading symbols and letters can make a great difference. Sensitivity to the need for larger print and larger images and pictures, and noting learners' problems in the classroom or in tutoring, can be vital to whether they stay or leave. If programs can find ways to help learners get to an optometrist to be checked for vision problems and help them afford eyewear, it can make all the difference between success and failure to some. Incidentally, most optometrists have a non-reader or "children's" eye chart available that uses symbols and pictures instead of lettering.

I said many will not be aware they are having vision problems. Years ago in a vocational college where I was teaching adult basic education, we had all of the ABE students come to the counselor's office and read the eye chart. I initially thought it was a waste of precious teaching time until I realized that about a third of our students needed glasses, and most of them didn't know it. Nor did we as teachers. We somehow managed to help most of them buy glasses through the program sponsors, but vision problems can present a major, unrecognized issue in literacy, basic education, and language programs. We often don't "see" what is in front of us.

"Sorry, but can we take a break?" If we as teachers feel tired, our adult learners will probably be feeling tired too. As Long (1983) states: "Teacher insensitivity to the reality of diminished energy levels can have negative consequences" (p. 29). Stretch breaks are important. I had a student recently introduce our adult class to a stand-and-stretch "energizer game." She led the class in spelling out words with our arms and legs. We found ourselves doing a hula-like movement for the "c," then the "o," and then bending down to make an "n" for the word: "coconut." It was hilarious. Other such energizers can involve having a student ask: "Did you had a cup of coffee today? If so, stand." Or, "Sit if you are glad the sun is shining this morning." "Touch your toes if you didn't do all of your reading homework last night." There are many ways to keep energy levels up besides going out for a "coffee and kidney break."

But the tried and true method of small group discussion is still one of the very best ways to keep the energy flowing. Likewise, posing problems for groups to solve, giving case studies for analysis, or having students engage in a "jigsaw" activity can be energizing. A jigsaw requires members of the class to engage with others in a pattern. For instance, some of the class members learn one aspect of a topic, some another aspect of it, and yet others master another. Two groups merge to share what they know. So Group A teaches Group B, and Group B teaches Group A. Meanwhile, Groups C and D are teaching each other. Then the groups change until every group has taught and learned everything involved from each other. Exercises like the "fish bowl," brainstorming, role play and countless others are discussed in some of the books on class activities as seen in the Reading List at the end of this chapter. A simple way to avoid diminished energy in any adult teaching setting is to have "volunteer energizers" in the group, students who volunteer to help the teacher look for signals of fatigue and ensure that breaks, physical stretches, and stimulating activities are being used to keep the energy up.

"I'm not feeling well." As Long rightly points out, adults often experience health problems, and "consideration of new information, creative problem solving, and reflective thinking can be reduced by medication despite the learner's heroic efforts" (Long 1983, p. 30). Here is an area where programs typically need to make some decisions. While issues around students' medication *should* come up during the intake period, and students *should* advise teachers when they have medication to control, for instance, epilepsy or schizophrenia or other health problems that may interfere with the learning process, in fact it doesn't always happen this way. In some literacy and ABE programs, the policy is that teachers and tutors need to be aware of who is on significant types of medication, and they are informed by the intake person soon after intake. Others have no such policies, since there are also real issues of student privacy involved.

However a program decides to address this needs to be handled, not ignored. Many learners will make heroic efforts to learn and attend class in spite of their health issues. But suffering in silence can be the worst of all scenarios, since even the most stalwart will eventually drop out if they can't manage due to health issues. Again, being aware that medication may be an issue when learners are not doing as well as they obviously should be and knowing what health issues your students are experiencing can be extremely important to learner success. Having a policy on this can make a big difference for all involved.

Knowing when to "Whoa": Coming right behind the last point is the issue of how much is too much. A point *not raised* by Long, and rarely noted in the mainstream adult education literature since our learners are so unique in so many respects, is that some adults who come to our programs will have been, and may still be, the victims of physical, emotional, and sexual abuse and violence (Horsman, 2000; Williamson, 2001). Literacy teachers need to know it is not a good idea to try to be a therapist. Instead, refer learners to the experts—and this relates to the medication point raised earlier. Who in the community or region can provide support and, on some occasions, shelter and safety? We are not psychiatrists, marriage counselors, drug counselors, and alcohol rehabilitation therapists all rolled into one. There are legitimate limits to teaching beyond which it becomes irresponsible—even dangerous—to go.

This can be handled if every literacy and ABE program has a list of local agencies and names of workers in those agencies on every teacher's or tutor's desk, or with the program counselor if there is one. We all should know when to refer students to the experts and what the protocol is to do this. Again, the best advice here is to have some guidelines for how to proceed when there are evident problems. There are limits to teaching.

LITERACY LEARNERS' WAYS OF KNOWING

The differences between our learners, children and mainstream adults now become more enigmatic as we enter the world of cognition. How people learn is a highly contested area (Merriam & Caffarella, 2005). We cannot discuss differences between adults and children without considering their most significant cognitive differences. Malcolm Knowles has helped simplify this complex area for adult educators with some clear statements that have actually shaped today's modern field of mainstream adult education. Knowles comes from the humanist approach to teaching, as seen in the last chapter and, while not all subscribe to the humanist philosophy, Knowles's following principles have held up well over the years for mainstream adult education. For our population, qualifiers are added, together with implications for our teaching.

1) Adults Grow From Dependency to Self-Directedness. The first principle that Knowles gives is that, as children become adults, "Their self-concept moves from one of being a dependent personality toward being a self-directed human being" (1980, pp. 44–45). As he explains it, "Children enter the world in a condition of complete dependency" (p. 45). As they grow, young children take on learning as their fulltime "occupation" (p. 45). Through time, their self-image develops and their sense of self-identity emerges as they *move ever towards more independence*. Now it gets very interesting.

As Knowles explains it, younger children are very often part of the planning and learning activities in kindergarten and in their early primary years but, "As children move up the educational ladder, they encounter more and more of the responsibility for their learning being taken by the teachers, the curriculum planner, and their parents" (1980, p. 45). Paradoxically, the experience of youth in schools, says Knowles, "freezes them into self-concepts of dependency" (p. 45). As a result, says Knowles, as young adults come out of school there is often need for a transition from the stage when they were used to being taught, to one where they are forced to be provider, or a parent, or an adult student, or a responsible adult citizen. Numerous professors, college faculty, and vocational education instructors will point out how their new students have the assumption that they are *to be taught*. This can be a real issue for literacy and ABE since self-directed learning, as Knowles argued, can so often seem like a foreign concept at the outset of adult education. As researchers such as Dan Pratt (1988) have found, an ease-in or "bridging" period from teaching to more self-directed learning may be necessary before most adults will feel comfortable and make the best use of individualized, open-ended program structures such as those typically found in post-secondary institutions.

What this means for us in literacy and ABE is that we often get those who drop out of school early and have suddenly found they have levels of responsibly thrust upon them far sooner than they might have wanted or ever imagined. It is hard for all young adults, according to Knowles, but even harder for so many of our learners; low education levels can result in low self-esteem, and new life roles often only exacerbate the usual problems. Knowles puts it this way. Irrespective of how old they may be when they come to our classes and tutoring situations, many of the adults "may carry over from their previous . . . schooling the perception that they are not very smart, at least in regard to academic work" (1980, p. 46). If we take Knowles's expectation of a need to be "taught" and combine this with our own learners' conflicted emotions toward past schooling—ranging from rage, to guilt, to shame—ours becomes a far more highly complex field than most other types of adult education.

Elsewhere (Quigley, 1987; Quigley & Uhland, 2000), I have written about research we did on the issue of dropouts from literacy and ABE programs. Our adult learners often have very mixed emotions about schooling, and I can remember some good examples of this from my own experience. I think of "Big Bill," a student in my very first ABE class in 1972. He told me what it was like at the age of 10 to still be in grade two, and what it was like when "they told me I was stupid for the last time." Asked what he did, Bill said, "I told them to 'shove it' and never went back." Bill was now an adult of my own age (although twice my size) filled with rage toward school and symbols of school—like me, his teacher. Bill had been labeled by the local teachers even before he arrived at his school because his older brothers and sisters had all been "problem kids." His family lived "on the wrong side of the tracks," and he felt they had to fight to make their way in a judgmental world of "the snobby educated." Bill strode into my classroom with a huge chip on his shoulder, but others entered feeling embarrassed or ashamed. I remember Laverna, a single mother of my own age, saying, "I come to school after dropping my 9-year-old daughter off at the primary school down the street. How humiliating!"

Despite the many ignominious experiences so many of our learners have experienced, we in literacy often expect a readiness for individualized, self-directed learning, and a level of eager "motivation" among our learners.

As cited earlier, Paul Jurmo makes the critical comment that, "Traditionally, literacy students have been handed a prescribed set of topics, materials, and activities that they are expected to master" (1989, p. 29). It was mentioned that many adult learners need a "transition" into self-directed learning. Ours very often need this transition. Deceptively, many of our adult learners will assume a passive behavior upon entering our programs; they may seem totally "dependent" in the first few days. But it is the context that often creates this posture, and it is the media and the centuries of "deficit perspective" that have helped create a public attitude that our adult learners are not really self-directed. Not real "adults" at all. Here's what Fingeret has said on this point:

> Educators believe that literacy is fundamental to competence and independence in modern society; it is difficult for us to conceptualize life without reading and writing as anything other than a limited, dull, dependent existence. As a result, adult basic educators continue to define their student populations in terms of incompetence, inability, and illiteracy, even though this kind of orientation has been labeled a "deficit" perspective and is under attack in a variety of social science disciplines. (1983, p. 133)

Thus, not all the implications of Knowles's first principle on self-image rest with our adult learners. They also involve us as adult teachers who need to be sensitive to the life transitions and frightening challenges we are seeing.

We need to remember that our learners can be experts in their own workplaces and communities. They can be respected and brilliant at their jobs or avocations. They can be gifted parents. They can have earned "a PhD in the school of life" but, instead, they are often seen as being in a "state of deficit," not only in the sense that they have limited reading, writing, and numeracy skills but in the sense that they can't possibly be complete, functioning adults.

Making this point painfully clear, here is what an ABE teacher in Massachusetts recently wrote me about one of her adult students: "Phil [fictitious name used] is a life long member of the small (pop. 6000) New England town [where I teach ABE]. He is a property owning, tax-paying resident who has worked steadily as a truck driver. Phil is a non-reader. He is 54 years old and told me that in second grade his teacher told him he was 'utterly stupid' and had him cleaning erasers. He told me he dropped out of school for good by fourth grade. He informed me that, 'I'd rather stand on a town hill, naked, and announce I am HIV positive than tell folks I can't read.'" (personal communication).

How can we deal with this situation in the classroom? Fingeret has explained that the more we know about the world of our own learners—the more we "become involved in the social networks of illiterate adults" (1983, p. 145)—the more we will know about and appreciate our learners' circumstances and their way of seeing the world. If we could see them in their real life, or at least have a positive appreciation of their own contexts and their own communities, we would find that most of our adult learners are highly independent, just as Knowles is saying. In many community-based situations, as Fingeret found, our adults often "see themselves as *inter-dependent* [italics added]; [since] they contribute a range of skills and knowledge other than reading and writing to their networks" (p. 134). While it is a stereotype to assume this fits every last one of our learners, and we have enough stereotypes already in literacy, Fingeret began her research believing what the media and much of the adult literacy literature at that time told her about low-literate adults. She went to communities in New York "expecting to find illiterate adults cut off from the social world, perhaps connected to the umbilical cord of television" (p. 135). However: "I began to observe a rich, highly interactive social world, co-existing with the harsh reality of the streets. Other adults were constantly stopping by to visit, to use the telephone, to offer a ride to the dairy, to pick up children being watched" (p. 135).

What This Means for Us in Literacy and ABE

Unlike teaching children, or even most mainstream adults, the challenge is to realize that many who come to our classrooms and tutoring sessions are accustomed to being *interdependent* in their own communities and among their peer groups. With this in mind, as seen later in this chapter, it is proposed we can build on interdependence in our classrooms with small group learning, support groups, group work within classrooms, problem-based activities for groups to work on, and learning activities that require collaboration among learners.

2) **A Growing Reservoir of Experience.** Knowles tells us in his second principle that adults "accumulate a growing reservoir of experience that becomes an increasingly rich resource for learning" (1980, p. 45). Time builds this reservoir of experience. Children have fewer life experiences to draw upon; therefore, effective adult educators will ensure that their adult learners have an opportunity to share and draw upon their experiences and will seek to make good use of this rich resource of experience in the learning-teaching process. As teachers, we often will relate our stories or experiences to make points. Learners should feel comfortable in doing so as well.

Here's a sad example with a happy ending. I was the GED administrator for my province in Canada when a man came in to see me. He was in blue overalls and explained that he was the supervisor of the maintenance staff of a multi-storied building complex visible from my own office window. His name was George, he had emigrated from Greece some 20 years ago, and he had failed his GED exam. He was in a state of near panic because, even though he had been in charge of a large crew of office maintenance and cleaning staff for more than two decades, if he did not obtain a GED high school equivalency diploma by the end of the year, he would be fired and replaced in his job by a high school graduate. All of his knowledge and skills through the decades were meaningless because he did not do well on this test. He wanted to know if the GED test was available in Greek. It is not.

After several highly stressful weeks of GED practice tests

with a tutor and yet another failed attempt at passing, George re-appeared at my door. Although the testing occurs in the colleges, he wanted to study in our mail room and became a permanent fixture for weeks. One day as he came in to "chat," I noticed he had a defect in his eye, and I asked about it. He said his vision was impaired in that eye. Inspirationally, I suggested he get a medical certificate so he could write the final test under the disability clause of the GED, which meant no timing limits. He entered the mail room with the third—and last allowable—version of the test sweating profusely. He wrote for days. When he finally emerged, he said a prayer in the middle of the office space, and left. The test was immediately scored. George passed! I don't know who was happier, George, me, or our GED secretary, who had taken the dozens of phone calls from George, his family, and his friends, all pleading, even threatening: "Just let George pass."

Knowles talks of a growing reservoir of knowledge but, for many of our literacy learners, society typically devalues their rich knowledge. Too many of our learners face endless injustices and indignities in their everyday lives because, like George, they only become "visible" if their own growing reservoir of knowledge is "validated" with a piece of paper.

What This Means for Us in Literacy and ABE

If we are to recognize the needs of our adult learners, we must first recognize "learner dignity" (Fingeret, 1989, p. 9). As Fingeret puts it, learner dignity is "at the heart of the belief that [adults with low literacy skills] . . . are not only able but . . . [have] the right to participate in creating programs that are supposed to serve their interests" (p. 9). The challenge for us, then, is to "recognize that non-reading adults are the creators of their own social lives, as imperfect as those lives may appear by middle class standards" (p. 9). Their knowledge and experiences should be recognized by teachers and tutors, as Knowles says, and put to practical use in helping develop and conduct programs that are, after all, intended to benefit their lives.

In order to see our learners as having valuable knowledge and dignity, we need to "understand that nonreading adults are not a homogeneous group. . . . The population of adults with low literacy skill levels is diverse, and it includes a large number of persons who have been consistently productive workers, family members, and in some cases community leaders" (Fingeret, 1989, p. 9; also see Reder & Green, 1985).

In summary, recognizing and employing adults' growing reservoir of knowledge begins with respecting the dignity of our learners and appreciating that we have a diversity of learners with much to contribute.

3) A Readiness to Learn. Knowles also tells us that adults' "readiness to learn becomes oriented increasingly to the developmental tasks of their social roles" (1980, p. 45). Therefore, learning needs to be relevant— relevant to the tasks that adults must deal with. In a foundational study conducted with approximately 2,000 mainstream American adults 25 years and older who were asked why they had returned to some form of mainstream adult education, "an impressive 83% of the learners surveyed described some past, present, or future change in their lives as reasons to learn" (Aslanian & Brickell, 1980, p. 50). Change often triggers the need to learn, or as the researchers put it, *transitions* draw adults back to formal education. A full 56% in this mainstream study named transitions in careers and job changes as the reason for returning to school. Let's consider the implications for literacy.

What This Means for Us in Literacy and ABE

There is no significant difference between this set of findings on why mainstream adults choose to return to education and reasons why most adults with low literacy skills return to adult basic and literacy education. Fingeret and Danin, for instance, found that ABE students' "decisions to enter the [ABE] program are not usually a response to one particular event, but rather part of a larger process of change in their lives" (1991,

p. 37). Again, transitions play a major role in the decision to re-enter the literacy education system, and the quest for a better career remains a major goal for many who come to our programs.

Therefore, if research puts an emphasis on the transitions phenomenon (e.g., Cross, 1982; Fingeret & Danin, 1991; Quigley, 1987), as educators we should expect our learners to have a high level of vulnerability when they enter the program simply because they are in a state of change and are typically experiencing a degree of uncertainty in their lives. Their life circumstances may only compound the fact that many of our learners come with highly emotional memories of schooling. Often they bring negative memories into the classroom or tutoring situations. Little wonder that attrition rates can be so high in our field, since "readiness to learn" is complicated for many of our students by ambiguous feelings towards school and profound vulnerability during the early weeks of our programs.

4) The Immediacy of Application. Knowles's fourth principle builds on the previous one. He says that adults' "time perspective changes from one of postponed application of knowledge to immediacy of application" (1980, p. 45). Unlike children and youth being told in school—and by their parents and adults outside school—that what they *must* learn will be of value *some day*, adults are "performance-centered" (p. 65). They seek learning that they can apply *now* and in the immediate future. In 1985, Knowles said, "Adults become ready to learn when they experience a need to know or do something in order to perform more effectively in some aspect of their livers" (p. 11). The key to the previous principle was relevance. Here it is immediacy.

Knowles has it right, according to a recent U.S. study that found that 46% of all American adults had participated in some type of formal or informal education in the previous 12-month period (Kim, Collins-Hagedorn, Williamson, & Chapman, 2004). This constitutes 92 million American adults in mainstream adult education. What were they coming to adult education to learn? A full 30% "participated in work-related courses and 21 percent participated in personal interest courses" (p. 15). In study after study, irrespective of whether it is formal or informal learning, adults seek practical knowledge when they engage in our educational activities. What we teach needs to be for use now—not years from now. "Some day" can be met with adults' voting with their feet.

What This Means for Us in Literacy and ABE

Just as physiological and sociological dimensions of working with adults are realities that influence success in teaching and tutoring, just as our learners are deeply affected by transitions, they need to feel that what they are learning will be actually useful, that it will solve problems—not create new ones.

5) **The Role of Motivation.** In 1985 Malcolm Knowles added a fifth principle. As he said, adults obviously "respond to some external motivators—a better job, a salary increase [but] . . . the more potent motivators are internal—self-esteem, recognition, better quality of life, greater self-confidence, self-actualization, and the like" (p. 12). This fifth principle is highly important for our work since it involves the enigma of motivation. In many literacy programs and much of the literature, the importance of enhancing learner self-esteem and self-confidence is discussed under this broad heading (e.g., Beder, 1991); however, I have come to think the better term is the one used extensively in New Zealand (e.g., Benseman, 2001). There, the discussion centers on building "self-efficacy," defined as "the sense of being able to perform some task or achieve some goal" (Bee, 1992, p. 512). No matter how it is defined, building learners' internal motivation to succeed in our programs can be the key to a learner's decision to stay or leave.

I remember two adult basic education teachers I supervised years ago when I was the ABE director in a community college. I'll call them John and Shirley. They co-taught, or more exactly they "co-coached" a life skills program of 16 weeks duration, never with more than 12 learners in the room. This was not an academic course. No books were used nor required. It wasn't about academics at all. Most of the students were referred to this life skills program from drug rehabilitation centers, local corrections' half-way houses, community Native Centers, and employment agencies. In almost every instance the professional counselors were at their wit's end. Everything that the professional counselors at those agencies had tried had failed. Incentives, rewards, threats . . . even imprisonment—it all ended up the same. From the agencies' perspectives, there was nothing that could be done with this group short of seeing them spend their lives on social assistance while going in and out of drug rehab centers and prison. John and Shirley's program was the last stop.

I remember a big sign that the two teachers had on their office wall: "We are not teaching subjects, we are teaching people." And did they ever do the job. I have seen many, many literacy and ABE teachers create a comfortable family atmosphere for learners—a first step that is vital in creating a positive learning atmosphere—but John and Shirley were way past positive climate-setting. This was as close to a therapeutic program as any I have ever seen. They strictly focused on learners' internal motivation. Esteem-building, confidence-building, and building self-efficacy made up the course content. Course after course, our follow-up statistics showed that over 80% got off alcohol and drugs and stayed off for at least 6 months. Over 60% got and held a job for at least a year. It was remarkable. As the ABE director, I would greet them when they arrived at the program and try to at least talk with them as they headed to the counselor, then to the classroom. Few were interested. Most were hostile, angry, distracted, feeling "sentenced to adult education." Some were coming off drugs and barely knew I was there. Yet virtually every graduate left saying he or she had a new life as a result of the program. I can attest to this fact, since most came back to tell us about their new lives, often with their children or families.

How did Shirley and John do it? They thoughtfully, skillfully and sincerely connected to those "more potent internal motivators" that Knowles talked about. With the group involved, they built "self-esteem, recognition, better quality of life, greater self-confidence, and self-actualization," as Knowles puts it. The learners re-gained their belief in their ability to perform some task or achieve some goal through enhanced self-efficacy. But it would be a mistake to think Shirley and John did this alone. If there was any magic involved, it came from the power of the peer group as tapped by the coaches. The peer group is an underutilized resource in the literacy classroom, one that will be returned to when we discuss a proposed interdependent model later in this chapter.

Let's take a look at what internal motivators and the preceding principles mean for us in our classrooms on a day-to-day basis.

NOW FOR SOME SPECIAL LITERACY CONSIDERATIONS

This discussion of five principles leads us to bring together the special challenges unique to our field—and our field is unique within adult education. For instance, when compared with mainstream adults, far fewer adults with low literacy skills participate in our sponsored programs. In study after study, we find that only about 8% of the potential number participate in ABE in the U.S. (Beder, 1994; Belzer & St. Clair, 2003). Compare this with studies that put mainstream participation into the 40% range and higher. It has been noted as well that ABE dropout rates typically range from 65% up to 80% (Quigley, 1997).

The facts are that all the research on participation and dropout in our field brings us back to "two major constellations of reasons" (Beder, 1989, p. 91) for low participation and high attrition rates. As Hal Beder explains, "One is structural; the other is attitudinal" (p. 91). These "constellations" of reasons, as originally developed by Pat Cross (1982), are often categorized as situational barriers, institutional barriers and dispositional (or attitudinal) barriers, as shown in Figure 4.1:

Let's consider these barriers for a moment. "Situational" refers to those deterrents that arise in the lives of our learners and in those of potential learners. Childcare issues, health is-

Situational Barriers

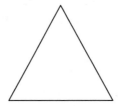

Institutional Barriers   Dispositional Barriers

Figure 4.1 Barriers to Participation and Learner Retention in ABE and Literacy

sues, family needs, issues around low income and poverty are a few of the examples that arise in the situations of their daily lives. These will all exist in mainstream adult education but not as acutely or as frequently. Institutional barriers are those we ourselves create and sustain. Examples include the geographic location of our programs, the "red tape" our institutions and those outside of ours can insist on, tuition costs, and the indirect costs of attending programs. Scheduling of courses and programs, access to public transportation. Dozens more can be added. Those with learning disabilities often find we have limited resources or access to learning specialists. While we often struggle to remove the barriers around our own programs, the sheer lack of budgets, constant program instability, and ingrained institutional traditions can all work against our best efforts.

Third, and where our field differs substantively from mainstream adult education, is in the area of attitudinal barriers, or what I have termed "dispositional barriers" (Quigley, 1997). This third area affects participation and attrition far more than our research has fully explored and requires a high level of professionalism in our teaching. How can we deal with these major barriers to participation and retention in our programs? Let's take a look at some possibilities.

HOW CAN WE ADDRESS OUR LEARNERS' SITUATIONAL BARRIERS?

If literacy and ABE teachers, tutors, administrators, and counselors have an understanding of learners' past and present circumstances—with an awareness of current transitions, needs and goals in their lives—we can get a reasonable grasp of both the situational barriers they face and the hopes they bring. Questions can be asked at intake, and *some* situational barriers will be revealed at that time. But only "some," since there will be students who will not be so quick to talk about their life or home problems. Being able to identify and deal with situational barriers as they get expressed and arise is an ongoing challenge for us. How can we deal with the situations that our learners may face in their lives? Here are two areas of suggestion:

Involving Community Agencies

We need to have a level of expertise in knowing when to offer help and when to refer to outside professionals and agencies. As touched on earlier, it is highly advisable that every practitioner in every program have a listing of the names and phone numbers of the key community or regional resource personnel in the community who can assist learners. Consider this: If a learner is subject to domestic violence, who would you call? And where and how would you refer the student? If a learner is having a medical problem or is suddenly ill, what are the next steps? Who do you contact in the program for help, and when do you act directly with an agency? What are your professional and legal responsibilities? This does not always have to be a crisis situation. What agencies or resources are available to *assist* with student learning disabilities that can be called upon or that a learner can be referred to for assistance until she or he is able to return? Learning differences can be a major gap in literacy and ABE instruction and comprise an important area to discuss in programs.

Learners Helping Learners

A largely overlooked resource for addressing at least some of the barriers that our learners face is other learners in the program. Very often learners will be glad to help other learners, if asked and if given some direction and parameters. Some of the possibilities are mentioned later, but introducing a "buddy-system" where issues and problems inside and outside the program can be discussed with a learner who is a friend or mentor, can be highly effective. Such pairing can be based on age difference—younger learners mentored by more mature ones or someone further along in the curriculum, for instance. Introducing group work in classrooms so there are groups of three, four, or five assigned to work together on a problem, including a real situational barrier issue, can be highly effective provided it is something that the group can help with. Introducing a self-help discussion group component to the program during or after the program hours can be very helpful. This will be taken up again later.

HOW CAN WE ADDRESS OUR LEARNERS' INSTITUTIONAL BARRIERS?

Institutional barriers can be the hardest for us to see because we are so surrounded by the everyday structure and systems of our programs that we often can't see our world through the eyes of our learners. Moreover, even when we do see the barriers created by our own programs, we often don't have the resources or the budget to do much about them. This doesn't mean we stop trying—just the opposite—but there are some direct ways we can address institutional barriers.

From the Inside Out

Many literacy and ABE programs could improve "from the inside out" simply by having teachers, tutors, counselors, and administrators *working more closely as a team.* Too many educators live in their classrooms or tutoring situations and communicate with other teachers and peers only on the most superficial level. It is hoped the learning circles arising from these chapters will help with this by creating a more collaborative culture around problems.

Student dropout is an example of a literacy problem that we typically can collaborate on more. Despite the fact that everyone is doing her or his best, it is often the case that the potential problems perceived or anticipated by the intake person at the "front end" of the program are not well conveyed to the teachers or tutors who will be working with those same learners. Or, if they are, the problems often lack a follow up set of suggestions or actions, including a way to give on-going group support and develop group decision making with the learners at risk of dropping out.

There are tests of field dependence and field independence that can be helpful in deciding on the support levels students may need (i.e., Quigley, 1997; Witkin, Oitman, Raskin, & Karp, 1971), and tests of self-concept (Beder, 1991), but as will be seen later in the interdependent model proposed for intake, one of the best and simplest predictors is simply to ask the students how well they think they will do in our program (and a guide is provided at the end of this chapter to help with this).

Such "asking" should begin with how the incoming students did in past schooling—both in each subject taught, and how well they felt they were supported, helped, and challenged by past teachers, past peers, and past counselors in school or past ABE programs. Within that framework, they can often make solid predictions on where their problems will reoccur in this program.

One Size Can't Fit All

If we are working as a team for the benefit of each learner and gaining different information on each learner, is it really necessary that every literacy and ABE student be treated in essentially the same way? Gaining information should tell us who needs more support, who needs less, who will probably do better—and stay longer if provided with alternative learning options. Why must the same set of intake and program procedures fit all students if all needs are not alike? One approach is to work more closely as a team for those who need more support—and "steal" the time needed for this extra support from those who need less. We actually do it in families all the time for the sibling or child who needs the most support.

To be critical for a moment, I have seen great success with the continuous intake and individualized program model used so widely in our field where students start regularly—perhaps weekly, even daily—and work according to a customized set of individualized activities in the classroom or on their own. But when I ask if this individualized model or the continuous intake system arises from asking students what the best learning system is for their needs, the answer is rarely that it was chosen because of what learners say they want or need. Having both administered and taught with this system, I sometimes wonder if it is sustained across North America more to keep student "flow through" and numbers high for statistical reports (I know because I too have found continuous intake to be a way to obfuscate reporting high dropout). But is this the best way? If we are to keep learners in the first few weeks, why not create more learning options in programs in the first weeks and beyond?

Having a "Safety Valve"

Research (Quigley, 1997) suggests that most students who are on the verge of dropping out will not discuss their thoughts with teachers or tutors, even their peers. Instead, some will go to a program person who is a "safety valve." This will be the intake person, the secretary, the janitor, or another teacher/tutor who has shown a special interest. This may actually be the last person to talk with a student who is thinking about dropping out—the student's and the program's last chance. In all

these cases, enhanced teamwork to help anticipate problems and
solutions can often turn the dropout rate around and make programs more successful for all involved, as seen later in the proposed model. Having some counseling or program training for
the "safety valve" in any program can be very helpful. Is there
a safety valve in your program?

HOW CAN WE ADDRESS OUR LEARNERS' DISPOSITIONAL BARRIERS?

While much can be done to improve learner success under
the categories of situational and institutional barriers, experience together with the literature on this topic tells us that most
of those who drop out will do so in the first 2 to 3 weeks
(Quigley, 1992). Why? Apart from those who are "court or-
dered" to attend and therefore can't (easily) drop out, research
indicates that the majority who come have organized their lives
sufficient to overcome short-term situational and institutional
barriers, or they likely would not be there. They have also built
up their resolve and walked up the steps to our program, but
why do so many walk back down within the first 2 to 3 weeks?
Beder (1994) has reported, "The dropout rate [is] 18% before
12 hours of instruction" (p. 16) in funded ABE programs across
the U.S. (also see Quigley, 1992, 1998). What happens in the
first two to three weeks involves the too often unseen *dispositional barriers* for many who decide to leave.

I believe it is here that we can make a far greater difference
in literacy. As Fingeret (1983) puts it: "Illiterate adults may feel
pressures to invalidate their perceptions of their own strengths
[given] . . . their understanding of how they are seen by members of the larger literate society" (p. 142). If we are to become
better at recognizing dispositional barriers, and provide choices
to those who otherwise will not do well in our program, here is
a proposed structure that especially focuses on the dropout issue
of the first 3 critical weeks.

DEVELOPING AN INTERDEPENDENT
LEARNING PROGRAM

From ABE to basic literacy tutoring, family literacy, workplace literacy, and literacy with second languages, there are many types of literacy programs and so many ways to structure them. Some work with "block intakes," or cohorts entering every few months. Some base their programs on one-on-one tutoring. Some work with families in drop-in settings. Some are organized after or, hopefully, during the work shift. But since continuous intake and individualized instruction are used so widely in adult basic education, what follows is a proposed model using a structure that I hope can be adopted or adapted to your situation.

In this model, new students are joining the program weekly, bi-weekly, or monthly, as is common in the continuous intake model prevalent in ABE and literacy. Further, the assumption here is that each student is given an individualized, customized program plan developed for her or him within the standard curriculum. This customized program will derive, it is assumed, mostly from a set of placement tests applied at intake and as supplemented by the teacher's own assessment(s). Students then work using their individual plan through "units" at their own speed by going to the program books, computers, reading lab materials, and other resource materials in the classroom as needed. The teacher acts as a resource person, giving an individual or group "lesson" as needed, but she or he mainly responds to individual problems. While this may look like the type of "learning contract" Knowles talked about, it is really not.

A PLAN FOCUSING ON THE FIRST
THREE CRITICAL WEEKS AND YOUR
PRACTICE PHILOSOPHY

First you will need an intake person. This person may in fact be one of the teachers or co-ordinators. She or he will provide a brief orientation and conduct placement testing on, for instance, every second Tuesday morning for new students. For this proposed example to be adapted to an interdependent model, there needs to be more than one teacher. There also needs to be other teachers, literacy volunteers, or student volunteers who can help in the intake period. This early phase in the program is seen as crucial and needs interdependent group effort.

Intake Day

- The intake occurs after lunch, at about 1:00 p.m.
- The orientation room has tables and chairs (as opposed to school desks) that can seat four to six at each table. The tables are arranged in a circle or in sets so that four sit at a table. As the new students arrive, they are greeted by the office receptionist, a teacher, or a volunteer, and are escorted to the orientation room.
- An intake of no more than 10 to 12 new students is best for this model.

The intake staff member or counselor then:

- Begins by setting a welcoming climate and provides some personalizing information about herself/himself; explains where the coffee, restroom, and smoke-break facilities are; and tries to set a low-stress climate while being cognizant that everyone in the group is an adult who should feel free to talk and ask questions. It is explained that this is an adult program where each learner will have a special, individualized program and will have the help she or he needs to succeed. *This isn't a school. It is a place where adults learn together.*
- The intake staff member explains that this program is collaborative in nature: "Students help other students here. We don't compete, we encourage everyone to work cooperatively — together and with the teachers/facilitators as well. It's a place where friends come; where everyone should be comfortable; where we would want to be."
- Allow for introductions around the group. This can be handled in many ways, but one is to have pairs where each student

interviews and introduces her or his partner (Name. Where they are from/born. What part of the city/area are they now living. What their goals are for the program. What their special interests are). The intake personnel should join in and be introduced by one of the new students, and the intake person should introduce her/his partner.

Then, take a tour of the facilities.

- Meet the teachers/facilitators and the support staff. Not just by looking in through the door, but by entering each room and moving around freely. Time the tour so they can see the learners at work and then, depending on the environment in the program, have the new students introduced to the current students and, possibly during a break period, have the new students meet the current ones on a more informal level. If they know each others' names before that break, it will help.
- Return to the orientation room and proceed with the help of other staff or students.
- Have one-on-one interviews with the new group of students using the "From the Past to the Future Intake Inventory" (at the end of this chapter). This will help reveal some of what the new students' past schooling experiences were like and where, in turn, they now expect their greatest challenges to be in this adult program. The results of this will be vital for on-going discussion and goal-setting through the next few weeks, and months.
- Following a short break, academic placement tests can be administered, possibly with the help of assisting staff or students, depending on the tests used.

    The intake is almost over, but it should be explained that the intake person and intake team will be available for consultation before the students head home: "If there is anything else to be discussed, anything you want to talk with us about, we can meet one-on-one now." What students need to bring the next day, their time schedules, and any other logistics can be repeated. Remind them that each adult learner will have a different program of study and a different type of learning program.

- Individual questions should be discussed as the new students go home for the day.
- The assessments, the placement tests, and the observations of the counselor and those who helped should be discussed *that same day* to determine if some of the learners might be better off with extra assistance and a supportive learning plan. Again, one size will not fit all. Here are four program learning alternatives that have been used with success *for those that are showing themselves to be obviously at risk for dropout.* I suggest making it a program challenge to see if the intake team can lower the dropout rate below that of the average dropout rate or, once this is all in place, beat the dropout rate of the previous intake (see the next chapter to make this into a research project).

1) Using a Supportive "Team Approach": Some learners will do better and stay in the program longer with a *supportive team approach*, especially those who have extra challenges and may need extra counseling support. This means giving concentrated follow-up by one or two of the intake team along with the students' teacher. It means these people will sit down weekly or twice a week for the first three weeks as a team, and with the student as appropriate at those times. They will review the student's progress, beginning with the baseline established in the "Past to Future Inventory" at the end of this chapter. They will think how to give this student all the academic and program challenge possible. *This could be the case for those new students with very poor schooling experiences, including poor experiences with peers or with teachers, or if they felt they were under-challenged—even "bored"—in school or previous ABE programs, which is often the case.*

2) Using a Supportive "Mentor Approach": A specific student "mentor," one who might assist in the program on a regular basis, can be very helpful for other at-risk students. *This might be the case if students indicate they are worried about the academic content and the individualized process in general. It can be a good way to bring younger learners into an adult setting by* *matching them with mature learners.* The supportive buddy or mentor can help the new student find materials and get around in the regular program, and can help out with content work and problems within the regular program. Both can benefit in the pairing. The idea of a self-help discussion group, perhaps at the end of the day, can be a good idea if there are a number of learners who seem to need to talk about their situational or other barriers.

3) Using a Supportive "Small Group Approach": Research (Quigley, 1997) conducted using these options indicated that small groups can be the best of all options for purposes of retention. But, it is not always possible to have a group of under 10 with a teacher—even if it would be ideal for some learners— but it can be possible to create learning groups within most classrooms. These can be based on certain subjects and by mixing the students based on levels. Let them learn using more of the progressive adult learning approach of problem solving. *This approach will prove most successful with those new students who are obviously in need of group-based peer support rather than student or counselor support. The intake instrument at the end of this chapter and the intake process itself will help with this decision.*

4) Using a Supportive "Tutor Approach": In some cases, a volunteer tutor available evenings, late afternoons, or weekends can make all the difference. It might be that a new student's schedule and situational barriers are going to be a problem. *If the intake team wonders if this person will come back each day, or if this new student seems to need extra academic assistance within or outside the program,* try assigning a helpful, well-trained volunteer to help. Again, community volunteers and student volunteers can play a large role in programs. Just being supportive after program hours and helping with homework can mean the new learner doesn't disengage.

5) No Extra Support: Simply place the student into the program with her/his customized curriculum with no extra help. *This is*

*for the more confident student who has no indication of dispo-
sitional or other barriers, including academic issues, and does
not appear to be at risk of dropping out in the first three weeks.*
Again, a team working together can cover for each other and
"steal" time from these same "persisters" who are able and willing to work with minimal assistance.

There may be other support options available to you in
your program. Ask yourself, "What can we do to reduce dropout, and maybe increase performance too, within the first three
weeks?"

Giving truly individualized help like this means it is important to discuss and analyze intake tests and interview comments
promptly after the intake so that new students can be placed the
next morning. The longer the waiting period to get situated, the
greater the chances are that new students won't return. Obviously, trying to have enough staff to help in the orientation and
work with learners in follow-up can be an organizational and a
resource challenge. Here's where volunteers can help—community and student—and, with some collected data (as seen in the
next chapter), where a case can be made for more part-time or
even full-time staff if attrition is to be reduced and performance
enhanced.

When the new students come back the next morning, they
should be met one-on-one. This again will require the help of
the intake team. The placement decisions and the suggested support options need to be discussed with each student. For some
who evidently will do better with more peer interaction and support, the small group setting may be suggested, the peer mentoring for others, explaining: "We want you to succeed. Based
on your past experiences and your goals, we're thinking more
contact with other students in a smaller group (or one-on-one
mentoring) might be worth a try." Remind them that they can
have this option reconsidered after a week or two by simply
coming back to an intake team member. They may be told that
a new arrangement might not be possible immediately, but a
different option will be accommodated as soon as possible. For
some needing in-program and outside help, the volunteer tutor
after hours or weekends may be suggested; for others, members

of the intake team might meet with them regularly and, working closely with the teacher, see how they are doing, and revisit their Past to the Future Inventory regularly to see how they are progressing.

The "Safety Valve"

As mentioned earlier, it is always good to have a "safety valve" available. Someone who is not their teacher or a peer whom they trust—like members of the initial intake team, a friendly teacher who has not been the student's own teacher, or the receptionist. In all cases, ensure there is a "last resort" possibility for them and that every student should know who is there to help beyond the student's teacher, and be comfortable enough to go for help should he or she be thinking of dropping out, or is in need of help.

THE FIRST CLASS MEETING

After each individual learning plan has been discussed with each new student, they should be escorted to their new classroom or small group setting and introduced, or re-introduced more exactly, to the teachers and students. The teachers should be given the findings and materials from the intake if they haven't already seen it (which would be ideal). The classroom teachers need to start working with the new students to make them comfortable in their new learning environment. Now, irrespective of the practice philosophy of the teacher, as seen in Chapter 3, (and see Vella, 1994; Wlodkowski, 1999), there are some suggested steps to further to help reduce dispositional barriers in the program and address early problems that can help with retention, as follows.

As discussed earlier, research on self-directed learning tells us that few adults are ready to "leap into" a self-directed program and be completely independent at the very beginning of a program of studies (i.e., Knowles, 1975; Pratt, 1988). An "ease-in" period is needed for most adults, especially our learners for all the reasons discussed earlier. The following plan assumes there are already a number of students in the classes, and these new ones are joining the class as part of a cohort intake.

1) Fostering Inclusion and Interdependent Learning:

OBJECTIVE	ACTIVITY
Create a welcoming classroom atmosphere	Introduce yourself and share something about yourself and about the group. Reinforce that *this is not school* and it isn't competitive: "We help each other learn and make learning useful and rewarding."
Build inclusiveness	Have the students introduce/re-introduce themselves. Again, you can ask the students to sit in pairs and interview each other—matching the new students with the ones already—to ascertain: "Your name?" "Where were you born?" "What area or part of the community do you now live in?" "What is your goal for this program?" "My past experiences with school and my hopes for this program are. . . . "
Create a climate of respect	Those student already in the class may then individually take turns explaining where they are in each of their course subjects, how far they have come on each, and their

timelines/goals for each subject. This can be drawn on a flip chart or the blackboard, or students can show the new students in pairs or in the group where they are in the various plans or books.

Encourage working together and collaborative learning

Ask the group to take up a class-based problem or question for discussion, have them form small groups to discuss the question, and then report back to the group. One suggestion could be to take a topic that is clearly of immediate concern to everyone, new students included, such as: "What are ways we can ensure that we all get here on time every morning?" Or, "What are ways we can help each other get here every day?" Have one group member report back ideas to the group.

Ensure that each learner's experiences and knowledge are valued

Next, based on the ideas brought back, all the students can discuss them if they want to develop some new classroom policies on, for instance, calling one another if someone needs a ride, or creating a phone tree to help those who have problems getting up early, or sharing child care in various communities. Ideas on how to take an issue that affects the whole class into a problem solving mode will be especially helpful.

Develop mutual respect by creating classroom policies and procedures that all learners own

Add what has just been decided to any policies the group has already in place and have the group review them all. Like a family, there normally need to be guidelines and rules everyone helps create and live by. Smoking rules, deciding on open-discussion topics on matters of concern, deciding on classroom speakers and field trips, developing a newsletter (see later suggestions) can all be ways to build collaboration and respect.

2) Building Interdependence:

A joke in adult education is: "We only know two things about adults: 1) adults love structure, and, 2) adults hate structure." They first want to know how the system works, and *then* they want to be able to move around in the structure, get exceptions from it, adapt it, and challenge it (in a nice way). Since we are still in the "phase-in" stage, a strong sense of group needs to be fostered, and if some of the suggested strategies discussed by the whole class are tried and adopted soon into the program, it will help. But expect some to ask for exceptions nevertheless.

Build a sense of the group as a learning resource

Students who have already said they are well along in certain subjects can help the new students with their math, science, English, reading, etc. This should just be a part of the regular day's activities. Explain that "Every learner has some special skills and knowledge, every student will help you, depending on what you need." Explain: "I'll be going over your progress with you regularly. Some have a tutor or will be working with the team approach; others here will be asked to be mentors. Some will be working on their own and need only ask me for help when they need it. We are all teachers and learners in this classroom; this is an individualized adult program that makes sure all learners get the help they need to do their best."

Maintain a sense of group engagement through bi-weekly discussions

On a regular basis, have a group discussion on a topic of interest and value to the group. These can be suggested by the group members or, for example, discussions can include:

- "What jobs are there in this area? How can we get into a meaningful career?" This could involve community speakers, tours, or placements.
- "How do we handle disci-

pline with our children
while showing them we
love them?" This could involve a professional from
a local agency.

- "How can we quit smok-
  ing? This could involve a
  professional from a local
  agency.

The first three weeks—the most critical ones for purposes
of retention—should have a high focus on the new students, and
staff should be especially concerned with keeping the students
in programs by noting and dealing with the three sets of barriers
discussed. The logic is, once the first hurdle of the first 2 to 3
weeks is overcome—the main dropout period—and a pattern
of interdependence is established, it will be time to more fully
build on the philosophy and special strengths you bring to the
classroom as the teacher or tutor. The program intake schedule
may need to be revised because, if the program attrition rates
are reduced, there will be fewer openings for new students. In
other words, it may not be the case that there are intakes every
two weeks; it may be that intakes will be based on openings
available. Or perhaps, if good data are collected (see the next
chapter), the argument might be made for new sections and
more teaching staff—a gratifying outcome if the proposed plan
is effective.

MOVING BEYOND INTAKE AND INTO OUR
OWN PRACTICE PHILOSOPHY

Since this guide is about professional development, the
needs and interests of the practitioner made up the first chapters
of the book. We have seen a section on the institution and the
learners' needs and strengths. Let's connect the two now and
look at how we can build a more solid foundation for sustained

professional practice that gives you more latitude for your own working philosophy.

After the First Three Weeks

Once the students begin to feel comfortable and are included in a group atmosphere that is Interdependent more than dependent or independent, your own philosophy can begin to set the tone and approach in the class. As noted before, there is never one way to teach adults, but you are the teacher and you should be using your strengths, interests, and gifts to make the classroom as vibrant and as meaningful as possible. You may choose to begin with one philosophical approach, and then bring in elements of another later. You may import teaching strategies from one philosophy to another. The student group, the funding agencies, or the program itself may lead you to emphasize one philosophical approach over another, but you should know what the choices are and why you have made them—here is a sign of a knowledgeable, professional teacher.

Let's turn to the weeks following the intake and phase-in, and look at the philosophy you are interested in.

PUTTING THE LIBERAL PHILOSOPHY OR THE VOCATIONAL PHILOSOPHY INTO PRACTICE

If you are inclined to teach with the liberal or the vocational philosophy, you'll probably agree that there is an important body of knowledge to be taught. From the Bristol School to the Port Royalists, from the teaching at Hull House to the Moonlight Schools and Frontier College, there was a body of knowledge that was to be taught. In both philosophies, the challenge is always to enable students to acquire and internalize important knowledge and necessary skills so that they may see things differently, act differently, behave differently, or reconsider the values and perceptions they brought into the classroom

(Mezirow, 1991a, 1991b). In no other philosophy seen here is Francis Bacon's maxim, "Knowledge is power," more applicable.

Learning Theory Involved

Approaching teaching from either of these perspectives may well involve a learning theory researched by David Ausubel (1968). In his watershed research, Ausubel wrote about "reception learning." This is where new concepts are added to one's existing knowledge—or cognitive structures. We use his idea of "advance organizers" all the time in teaching so learners can have a clear picture of what is to come each day or each lesson, along with what is expected in advance. Handouts, outlines, or course overviews given in advance of the new learning are all good examples of advance organizers.

For us in literacy, the challenge of both philosophies is to make them stimulating and as relevant to learner needs as Knowles would suggest. So much depends on the teacher in these philosophies. Here are some suggestions, but the ideas here can be transported into any of the other philosophies as well.

Cornerstones of Excellence

Since the teacher is vital to the success of these approaches, we need to begin with the very notion of what Wlodkowski (1988) calls excellence in the teaching of adult learners. He gives us four cornerstones of excellence: "Expertise, empathy, enthusiasm, and clarity" (p. 17). These will be referred to several times in the suggestions seen below so they come clearer in context.

Setting the Example

"Reception learning" lends itself very well to our programs. We typically expect the learners to work through the materials on their own in a standard individualized program of instruction. But it isn't enough to say the content *should* be sufficiently interesting unto itself to sustain interest. Learners sometimes drop out of our programs because they simply get bored (Fingeret & Danin, 1991), and it can be too easy to blame them for not seeing the "value of the content." So we can set an example using the liberal or vocational approach. How?

First, we absolutely need to know our subject—that is, we must have the *expertise* and convey it with *clarity* in plain language so it is understood by all. And the liberal and vocational absolutely demand high levels of content knowledge and clarity. But as Wlodkowki (1985, 1999) in his four cornerstones would agree, *nothing enthuses like enthusiasm*. If we are bored by our own subject or topic, what can we expect from our learners? Few have made this point better than Wlodkowski himself. He tells us: "Allowing ourselves to be emotional about what we teach is the key" (1985, p. 33). Adding: "Getting excited about new concepts, skills, materials, and future events related to our subject; showing wonder about discoveries and insights that emerge from our learners; and sincerely expressing feelings about the things we do with our learners" (p. 33) means we can lead by example.

In literacy and ABE, there is so much room for enthusiasm and for setting an example on clarity and expertise, because most of our learners are so highly skilled in orality. This means that many are comfortable with spoken stories, anecdotes, and humor, and most will rise to discuss, debate, and make conversation if they are encouraged. Literacy classrooms are typically filled with printed material; as a result, it may be hard for learners to be comfortable in classrooms surrounded by print. They can't be expected to feel as safe in such spaces as we do. For teachers, print is often a comfort; for learners it has long been a threat or a "task."

How comforting, even magical if, just for a short while, learners can sit back and hear short stories, or "inaccessible" novels raised from the printed page and put into the spoken word, or poetry by the students or by other poets read aloud. With our adults, a good learning environment encourages space for speaking, listening, and laughing. It is vital to give our learners time to look up from the books and feel they are still actually learning using the spoken word.

A last important point is the key term used by Wlodkowski. He said: "*sincerely* expressing feelings about the things we do with our learners" (1985, 1999) [italics added] is important. All our efforts around expertise, clarity, and enthusiasm will ring hollow if we are working from a deficit perspective. Experience has taught me that our learners often have an acute sensitivity to our attitudes, our body language, and the signals we project in the classroom. Again, the more we know about the learners' background and goals, the more we can *empathize* with and take sincere delight in the everyday victories of our learners. Of the four cornerstones of excellence, I would suggest empathy is the first and most fundamental one for us in the literacy field. It has been our touchstone through history, after all.

Owning the Learning

Our learners can quickly become disengaged if there is little or no sense that they "own the learning" and are removed from it. If we offer pedantic schooling and make it a drudge, we will see them drop out in the first three critical weeks. Based on Knowles's principles, the content will be far more interesting to learners if it is seen as relevant and needed by learners. Knowing the interests, backgrounds, and goals of our learners, and being *empathetic* to what they are attempting to achieve can be so important in making the content relevant.

Specifically Vocational

Looking now at this from a more vocational approach, students will find their literacy and ABE subject content far more interesting if the materials and the examples used arise from the occupations they are seeking to enter. Of course, there may be students in the classroom not looking to enter the workforce, but they might have family members or friends seeking to join it, or they might be interested in moving into certain areas or occupations later in life. We need to know about their lives and their dreams; the intake can help with this, as can the inventory offered at the end of this chapter. Through the small group and mentoring systems noted earlier, students can help others see how certain topics are relevant to them; thus, *enthusiasm* can be catching if given the chance.

Finally, if our students' growing reservoir of experience is tapped into for the vocational philosophy, as Knowles recommends, then individual students or groups of students can be asked to develop real-life problems arising from the course content, or help create real-life case studies to discuss or problem solve. Inviting guest speakers, bringing in content material directly from the workplace of the occupations of interest, identifying job tasks, purchasing resource books concerning those occupations, and adding videos about the workplaces of interest are just some ways teachers can generate the relevant vocabulary and setting. Tours to the jobsites and workplace time spent volunteering on the job can be extremely helpful as a conclusion to the course.

Critical Thinking

Many will agree that critical thinking needs a more dominant place across literacy and ABE teaching. Stephen Brookfield (1988, 1990, 1995) has argued that critical thinking is important in all mainstream adult education because it is "one of the intellectual functions most characteristic of adult life" (1990, p. 20). Compellingly, he adds: "It is necessary for personal survival" (p. 20). This is especially true for our learners, since most literacy and ABE teachers will say many of our learners have had problems or have been victimized because they just aren't astute enough in critical thinking. Taken from Brookfield's point of view, they are not seeing, for instance, systemic racism or institutional oppression that so often is interpreted as my "personal failing." We need to "aim to nurture in students a critically alert, questioning cast of mind," as Brookfield says (p. 24). This cast of mind "entails a readiness to scrutinize claims to universal truths with skepticism, to reject monocausal explanations of complex issues, and to mistrust final solutions to intractable problems" (p. 24). Critical thinking is one of the foundational beliefs within a liberal education and is highly important to the other philosophies as well. For vocationalism, it is certainly one of the first concerns of employers in the 21st century (Marsick, 1988). Techniques for developing critical thinking in adult learners have been well documented elsewhere (e.g., Brookfield, 1988, 1991), but above all, as Brookfield insists, this time-honored way of thinking can be modeled by setting an example as a critically reflective teacher ourselves.

PUTTING THE PROGRESSIVE AND RADICAL PHILOSOPHIES INTO PRACTICE

The progressive and radical philosophies have much in common. They do not begin with a canon of knowledge and skills that need to be learned; they begin by asserting that the process and the outcomes, not the "received knowledge," are what really matter. The Antigonish Movement is the clearest example of this, but there was room for this in the Frontier College and Hull Hull House curricula. Learners and teachers together can pose problems, bring real life problems, and solve problems; they can *create* knowledge and skills as well as *acquire* them. Unlike the earlier reception learning approach, we don't know precisely where we will come out, we are not precisely sure of how we'll get there, but we all understand that "learning by doing," as Kurt Lewin said, helps internalize learning and becomes part of us.

Learning Theory Involved

Understood from the point of view of learning theory, the progressives and radicals find their theoretical roots in what Jerome Bruner called "discovery learning" (1965). As Bruner explained in his classic research, to learn by discovery is a fundamental, natural, and lasting way to "own" the learning. It is "finding-out-for-oneself" (p. 608) and consists of "rearranging or transforming evidence in such a way that one is enabled to go beyond the evidence . . . to additional new insights" (pp. 607–608).

The educational strengths of the progressive and radical philosophies are many. They both can foster "particular ways of thinking or problem solving" (Pratt, 1998, p. 46). How? By actually participating in learning. As Bruner put it: "The student is not a bench-bound listener, but is taking a part in the formulation and at times may play the principal role [in the learning activities]" (1965, p. 608). For the progressive approach, this includes practical problem solving and ways to analyze and think our way through issues. For the radical, it typically means raising consciousness, building skills of critical analysis, and acting to address social injustices and problems such as sexism, racism, ageism, and issues arising from sexual orientation, income, and class. Irrespective of how problems are posed, identified, or how deeply critical they are addressed or acted upon, discovery learning can lift interest in the classroom in ways a single teacher's efforts cannot. It reduces the "performance expectations" of the teacher that can be so challenging in the liberal and vocational approaches by adding the learners to the full learning processes involved. Used consistently to its logical end, it ultimately makes the teacher "unnecessary," since the learning process is slowly taken over by the learners. It is "teaching with the lid off."

Thinking back to the first part of this chapter, discovery learning in the progressive and radical streams of philosophy provides countless opportunities to advance critical thinking. Discovery creates an atmosphere of challenge—even frustration—so questioning can go in all directions, including inwards towards one's own beliefs. But it can also be disconcerting for those learners who are far more comfortable being "taught," and it can be uncomfortable for the teacher who is used to having a set agenda developed for "reception learning." Teaching style matters here, and you may well prefer to use these approaches only on occasion depending on the topic and the group.

One downside in this approach is that discovery requires a good knowledge of what learners already know and the ways

they process information. In some cultures, it will fall flat—
at least initially. These approaches typically appeal to North
American and Western adults. In our classrooms and tutoring
situations, this approach may well require the "reawakening"
of curiosity and the confidence of some of our learners to seek
new answers alone or in groups. It also requires confidence in
ourselves as teachers.

But now here's the real downside: Discovery learning requires more time to plan and conduct than it may initially appear. Discovery is a carefully orchestrated investigation leading
to an anticipated—but not controlled—end point. Teachers who
are confined by 45-minute class time schedules, for example,
will need to think about how to carry problem solving activities
over more than one class meeting—perhaps over an entire term.

Finding the Problem: Knowing the Purpose

If your program follows an interdependent instruction model,
or even if it does not, it is possible to turn many of the content
lessons in the individualized materials towards discovery—that
is, to turn content toward problem-solving questions. Clearly,
different problems require different responses and different types
of thinking. Before setting out with this, ask yourself: "What
am I seeking here?" "What am I really looking for?" It may help
in this to know that White and Gunstone (1992) tell us that
problem-based questions that begin with "Why," "How," and
"What if" will elicit probing and reflection. Those that open
with "What," "Who," "Where," or "When" will typically encourage recall of information. So, first ask, are you seeking: 1)
direct recall; 2) a problem-solving requirement for researching
and applying information (on the internet or in books, for example); 3) or judgment and reasoning—as is required in the
GED exams? On a more sophisticated level, are you seeking 4)
to employ all of these skills by challenging students to rethink
their assumptions and prior knowledge? So before using the discovery approach, it is important to consider what you want to

achieve, how this may build on other learning activities, and the depths of criticality and activity you are looking for.

Let's now extend this further into the radical philosophy.

Naming the World

Paolo Freire tells us: "To exist humanly is to name the world" (1970, p. 76). From this perspective, the role and responsibility of the teacher is often to facilitate the "naming" toward an ultimate reconsideration of the world and how it functions. There can be powerful transformative dimensions to this philosophy that builds critical reflectivity. Often, facilitators from this perspective focus learning on relevant problems arising from the learners' lives, and many of those, in turn, will deal with areas such as race, gender, sexual orientation, class and, for many in our classrooms, prejudices that arise from a lack of a formal education. Here, learners are encouraged to exercise their right to speak for themselves, their families, and their communities; they are encouraged to see that the circumstances they might find themselves in arise from social inequities and prejudices. Problems are not always "their fault."

Transforming ways of seeing the world is a time honored philosophy in literacy education around the world, but like the other philosophies, there are certain consequences that typically go with this approach. Author bell hooks reflected on her teaching in a university setting, saying: "The presence of tension—and at times even conflict—often meant that students did not enjoy my classes or love me, their professor, as I secretly wanted them to do" (1994, p. 42). Nevertheless, it was worth it, she says, since: "I have found through the years that many of my students who bitch endlessly while they are taking my classes contact me at a later date to talk about how much that experience meant for them, how much they learned" (p. 42).

This approach will raise issues that are under the surface and can unquestionably be emotionally-charged. Taking this road involves *empathy, clarity, enthusiasm, and expertise*, but once again be aware of what the purpose is. What are you trying to accomplish? How will you evaluate it? How far are you prepared to go with the issues affecting learners?

We turn now to the philosophy that many in this field would agree is a major part of their personal practice philosophy.

USING THE HUMANIST PHILOSOPHY IN LITERACY AND ABE TEACHING

As T'Kenye (1998) argues: "It is easier to focus on content or on skillful presentation and assume that a high percentage of passing grades indicates teaching success" (p. 158). For the humanists, grades are not nearly enough. Instead, as Knowles has stated: "The deepest human need is for self-esteem, and . . . each of us has an obligation to help one another achieve it and maintain it" (1980, p. 87). This philosophy seeks to teach from *where the adult learner is*, rather than where the learner *should be*. Let's now consider the challenges and benefits of this philosophy.

Mutual Planning

The earlier discussion of the first class meeting and phase-in period, if adopted or adapted, can set the stage for mutual planning in the classroom and, in essence, we see in it a humanist approach in the interdependent intake since each learner's needs have clearly come before the needs of the institution, the teachers, or the funding agencies.

Knowles and others who have written from this philosophy, such as Fingeret and Jurmo (1989), and Jane Vella (1994), all argue that the key to the humanist approach is not simply a caring teacher but "self-diagnosis" (1980, p. 232). Among the four cornerstones of excellence, empathy becomes the first among equals. The Intake Inventory at the end of this chapter can help start the process, and so can program placement tests—

including teacher-made and learner-made placement tests. Furthermore, Knowles has given suggestions for developing a self-directed learning plan (1975, 1980, pp. 386–389) which might be of some help using this approach. If the longer term goals and milestones along the way are derived from the learner's past experiences, and if mutual expectations for progress are built around present possibilities in the program, the focus can be put on future short-term objectives in 2- to 3-week objectives. In other words, short-term objectives can build academic and personal confidence quickly and make distant goals like the GED or other completion points more attainable.

Evaluate Individual Competencies, Not "Standardized Levels"

A valid question in this philosophy is: "How can we have a program based on individual needs? Won't this be chaotic?" Some will say: "Surely we need common standards throughout a program?" For T'Kenye (1998), the answer lies in rethinking many of the myths around standardization. If we put more evaluation emphasis on "competency levels rather than performance levels" (p. 160), then individual differences should be expected, and progress can be measured based on how well math competencies, reading competencies, and writing competencies are being attained based on where each individual started. The Intake Inventory can play a part here. Try saying to your student: "Look at your progress in math on your intake inventory compared with how things went back in school." Or, "Look how well you are doing in the classroom (or in the tutoring situation) compared with how well you said you got along with the teacher and others back in school." Adult education attendance goals, goals for working with peers, goals in effectively working with the teacher are all on the inventory at the end of the chapter, and all can all be part in achieving short-term, comparable competency levels. Even elusive self-esteem can be compared to past schooling by using this approach. "Performance levels" and standardized levels may set workable norms for the institution and give a common language for administering purposes, but are they actually relevant to learners' stated needs and objectives? In the humanist approach, self-diagnosis can show competencies. Comparing today's competencies to past schooling can be a good starting place. Let students measure themselves more in the humanist approach.

Learning Inside and Outside the Program

Once the learner's individualized study plan and learning supports are in place during the early weeks, along with ways to measure competencies, learners can be encouraged to build their skills and knowledge in the group, and *outside the program* if they "help their children or grandchildren to deal with literacy-related tasks" (Jurmo, 1989, p. 30). The vastly underused approach of students volunteering in the community or in the program itself by, for instance, helping train new board members and program staff or, as will be seen in Chapter Five, participating in program research, is one way learners can put skills to use, add knowledge, and enhance self-efficacy and personal values.

Is Teaching Over-Rated?

More than 20 years ago, one of the founders of humanism, Carl Rogers, said: "Teaching is a vastly over-rated function" (1983, p. 151). The concept behind humanism is learning, not teaching. What Jane Vella calls "honest dialogue" (1994, p. 190) and the willingness "to listen, to learn, to grow out of our own roots" (p. 191) is vital to fostering learning. We "teach" no one, we only encourage them to learn. But the two "downsides" of humanism are, first, how do we set uniform standards, consistencies, transferability, and meet funder's expectations with humanism? Secondly, it can well be argued that all learners are not as eager to help plan, evaluate, even participate in our programs as the humanist authors may want or expect. If bell hooks found some of her students didn't "love her" in the radical approach, some teachers may find the "zone" of humanism too close for how they want to relate to learners (Quigley, 1987).

It always comes back to an informed decision on the practice philosophy that you want to develop and build upon. Knowing the strengths and limits of your philosophy, as well as what we can "borrow" from the philosophy options, is vital to building professionalism.

The following questions will help you and your co-learners reflect on what we have seen in this chapter, and give you a chance to bring your own ideas into the learning circle.

CHAPTER 4 DISCUSSION TOPICS FOR CONSIDERATION IN YOUR LEARNING JOURNAL AND LEARNING CIRCLE

- Do you agree with the sociological considerations as presented on how adults differ from children when it comes to our learners? Does this ring true?
- Do you agree with Long's observations about adults and the physical aging issues adults bring to our teaching? Are there other age-related aspects that apply to our learners not mentioned here? And are there other strategies you know of to address them?
- What does your program do about the question of students and medication? Do teachers and tutors know about significant medication issues of certain students? Should they? How is student privacy handled in these cases?
- What about Knowles' five principles on how adults learn for purposes of teaching and learning? Do these "fit" our learners, as discussed? What other principles should we be adding to these?
- What about the younger adults who come to your program? Do the principles and implications still apply? What have you found to be successful strategies in order to integrate and

teach younger adults with the more mature adults in the same classroom?

- Three barriers identified in the research and the ways they affect our learners were discussed. How do each of these barriers affect the students you have taught? What strategies have you found that should be added to the discussion on barriers?
- Student dropout was named as one of the largest, most pressing issues in ABE and literacy education. How serious is attrition in your program?
- Which of the suggestions listed here might be worth trying in your program to address student attrition? What other ideas do you have for dealing with dropout?
- The continuous-intake, individualized program model was used for the example given. Would the interdependent program approach, *or aspects of it*, work in your program or tutoring situation? If so, how?
- Does the concept of student "phase-in" seem to be important? How do new students get acclimatized, and how do they phase into your classroom or tutoring now?
- Do the suggestions for implementing the five practice philosophies seem to be workable for you? Will you try any of them? What other suggestions would you have for implementing your philosophy?

* To see if changes in your practice actually make an evidence-based difference and are successful, it is suggested you create an action research project, as discussed in Chapter Five.

CHAPTER 4
ACTIVITY OPTIONS FOR FOLLOW-UP

1) Look back through your learning journal and make your entries from this chapter. What, if anything, has changed in your thinking about teaching adult learners? Your approaches to teaching adults? Has anything changed concerning the ideas you might now try in your classroom or tutoring situation? Comment on these in your learning journal and discuss your observations in your learning circle.

2) In the classroom, consider one or more "tests" to see if vision, hearing, health and other issues of aging are actually factors in your classroom. Try an "eye-chart test" or a "hearing test" with your students. Consider involving health professionals or reading specialists to see if physical/cognitive issues actually are significant factors in the classrooms. However, think first about how these will be addressed if problems are revealed. What are your program's resources and what are your agency's referral options?

3) Discuss Long's and/or Knowles's principles in your learning circle. Discuss them with your adult learners. Is there a difference of views between your colleagues in your circle and your learners on these stated principles?

4) Discuss the three barriers with your co-learners and/or the learners. Do they agree with them? Do the two groups differ in their response to the three barriers?

5) Based on your practice philosophy and possible interest in other philosophies, consider trying some of the critical thinking techniques described in the resource books (seen next in the sources list). To test the success of this or other approaches from the various philosophies, maybe try an action research project (see Chapter 5).

6) Try some or all of the suggested aspects of the interdependent program to see if they improve retention, learning, and classroom atmosphere overall (again, to measure success, see Chapter 5).

CHAPTER 4: FURTHER READING

On Teaching Mainstream Adults with Application to Literacy and ABE:

Hiemstra, R., & Sisco, B. (1990). *Individualizing Instruction*. San Francisco: Jossey-Bass.

Knowles, M. (1980). *The modern practice of adult education*. New York: Cambridge.

Vella, J. (1994). *Learning to listen, learning to teach*. San Francisco: Jossey-Bass.

Wlodkowski, R. (1999). *Enhancing adult motivation to learn* (Rev. Ed.). 1999). San Francisco: Jossey-Bass.

On Teaching ABE and Literacy Adult Learners:

Dirkx, J., & Prenger, S. (1997). *A guide for planning and implementing instruction for Adults*. San Francisco: Jossey-Bass.

Fingeret, H., & Jurmo, P. (1989). *Participatory literacy education*. New Directions for Adult and Continuing Education No. 42. San Francisco: Jossey-Bass.

On Teaching Critical Thinking and Developing Critical Reflectivity:

Brookfield, SD. (1988). *Developing critical thinkers: Challenging adults to explore alternative ways of thinking and acting*. San Francisco: Jossey-Bass.

Brookfield, S. (1995). *Becoming a critically reflective teacher*. San Francisco: Jossey-Bass.

Cranton, P. (2003). *Finding our way*. Dayton, OH: Wall & Emerson.

For Group Process and Facilitation Ideas:

Heron, J. (1999). *The complete facilitator's handbook*. Sterling, VA: Kogan Page.

Leypoldt, M. (1967) *40 ways to teach in groups*. Valley Forge, PA: Judson Press.

Silberman, M. (1990). *Active training: A handbook of techniques, designs, case examples, and tips*. New York: Maxwell Macmillan International

FROM THE PAST TO THE FUTURE:
LITERACY/ABE INTAKE INVENTORY

Staff Copy

INSTRUCTIONS FOR THIS INVENTORY

This instrument effectively "begins" the student's program by having the new student think back and recall experiences of past schooling. It then guides you to ask how the student thinks she/he will do in the literacy/ABE program being considered. It therefore uses a comparative approach—past to future. Future progress can then be measured against this baseline discussion on each of the topics below.

This intake inventory is designed to be used, one-on-one, by a literacy or ABE counselor, or trained literacy/ABE practitioner, during the intake or orientation period of an adult literacy or ABE program of study. To accommodate lower reading levels, it is designed to be read aloud, statement-by-statement, by the intake person. The incoming student should also have a copy of this inventory. The student should respond to each question by circling the appropriate number with a pencil. Note: *the larger the size of the number, the stronger the agreement.* This inventory should be adapted to accommodate the subject names used by the institution or program (see questions 5 and 6). Additional discussion that arises from the questions can also be noted by the intake person on a separate sheet.

To Be Read Aloud by the Intake Person

Date _____

| **Learner's** | **Intake** |
| **Name** _____ | **Person's Name** _____ |

1 = A very negative "No" 1 ← → 7 = A very positive "Yes"

1. An education is very important to me   1 2 3 4 5 6 7
at this point in my life.

2. When I think back <u>to my past school experiences</u>:

   • The teachers were helpful.   1 2 3 4 5 6 7

And when I think about <u>the adult education program here</u>:

   • The teachers here will be even more   1 2 3 4 5 6 7
   helpful here.

3. When I think back <u>to my past school experiences</u>:

   • The counselors and staff were helpful   1 2 3 4 5 6 7
   then.

And when I think about <u>the adult education program here</u>:

   • The counselor and staff will be even   1 2 3 4 5 6 7
   more helpful here.

4. When I think back <u>to my past school experiences</u>:

   • My friends in the school were helpful   1 2 3 4 5 6 7
   then.

And now, thinking about <u>the adult education program</u> here:

   • I think my new program friends will   1 2 3 4 5 6 7
   be more helpful here.

5. When I think back to <u>my past school experiences</u>:

   • My family and friends at home were   1 2 3 4 5 6 7
   helpful.

And now think about <u>the adult education program here</u>:

- My family and friends will be even   1 2 3 4 5 6 7
  more helpful here.

6. Looking at the subjects I will be studying:

- I did well in math <u>back in school</u>.   1 2 3 4 5 6 7

- I will do better in math <u>here</u>.   1 2 3 4 5 6 7

- I did well in reading and English back   1 2 3 4 5 6 7
  in school.

- I will do better in reading and English   1 2 3 4 5 6 7
  <u>here</u>.

- I did well in science <u>back in school</u>.   1 2 3 4 5 6 7

- I will do better in science <u>here</u>.   1 2 3 4 5 6 7

- I did well in social studies <u>back in</u>   1 2 3 4 5 6 7
  <u>school</u>.

- I will do better in social studies <u>here</u>.   1 2 3 4 5 6 7

7. I made friends easily back <u>in school</u>.   1 2 3 4 5 6 7

- I will make friends more easily <u>here</u>.   1 2 3 4 5 6 7

8. I expect to do better <u>in this program</u>   1 2 3 4 5 6 7
<u>than in school</u>.

9. My greatest concern coming into this program is   _____

_____

(student or intake person to fill in)

10. My best idea for overcoming this during the program is __

_____

(student or intake person to fill in)

(adapted from Quigley, 1997)

FROM THE PAST TO THE FUTURE:
LITERACY/ABE INTAKE INVENTORY

Student Copy

Date _____

Learner's   **Intake**
Name _____   **Person's Name** _____

1 = A very negative "No" 1 ← → 7 = A very positive "Yes"

1. An education is very important to me   1 2 3 4 5 6 7
at this point in my life.

2. When I think back to my past school experiences:

   • The teachers were helpful.   1 2 3 4 5 6 7

And when I think about the adult education program here:

   • The teachers here will be even more   1 2 3 4 5 6 7
   helpful here.

3. When I think back to my past school experiences:

   • The counselors and staff were helpful   1 2 3 4 5 6 7
   then.

And when I think about the adult education program here:

   • The counselor and staff will be even   1 2 3 4 5 6 7
   more helpful here.

4. When I think back to my past school experiences:

   • My friends in the school were helpful   1 2 3 4 5 6 7
   then.

And now think about the adult education program here:

   • I think my new program friends will   1 2 3 4 5 6 7
   be more helpful here.

5. When I think back to my past school experiences:

- My family and friends at home were   1 2 3 4 5 6 7
  helpful.

And now think about the adult education program here:

- My family and friends will be even   1 2 3 4 5 6 7
  more helpful here.

6. Looking at the subjects I will be studying:

- I did well in math back in school.   1 2 3 4 5 6 7

- I will do better in math here.   1 2 3 4 5 6 7

- I did well in reading and English back   1 2 3 4 5 6 7
  in school.

- I will do better in reading and English   1 2 3 4 5 6 7
  here.

- I did well in science.   1 2 3 4 5 6 7

- I will do better in science here.   1 2 3 4 5 6 7

- I did well in social studies.   1 2 3 4 5 6 7

- I will do better in social studies here.   1 2 3 4 5 6 7

7. I made friends easily back in school.   1 2 3 4 5 6 7

- I will make friends more easily here.   1 2 3 4 5 6 7

8. I expect to do better in this program   1 2 3 4 5 6 7
than in school.

9. My greatest concern coming into this program is _____

_____

(student or intake person to fill in)

10. My best idea for overcoming this during the program is __

_____

(student or intake person to fill in)

(adapted from Quigley, 1997)

CHAPTER 5

"Creating Our Own Knowledge, Claiming Our Own Future"

Seek first to understand. Before the problems come up, before you try to evaluate and prescribe, before you try to present your own ideas—seek to understand. It's a powerful habit of effective interdependence.

—Stephen Covey

Ours is a field built on caring and sustained with compassion. Whether teaching, tutoring, administering, or counseling, we share the trials, the triumphs, the life transformations of our learners. The personal rewards are many but, as Fingeret and Danin (1991) have put it, "Simply working with a caring individual is not sufficient" (p. 90). So much of what we do in adult literacy is from the heart—but it takes more than heart to build a profession. In Chapter 1 we saw how the component parts of knowledge, skills, and values might be visualized as a metaphor whereby values could be thought of as the heart, knowledge as the head, and skills as the hand (Lander, 1996). With this interconnected, body metaphor in mind, our field has a strong heart. And as we've seen throughout our history and today, many practitioners and programs have countless skills—skills "of the hand" too often under-recognized and undervalued. Likewise, there is enormous practice knowledge in our field which is undervalued, inadequately documented, and poorly disseminated. It is hoped the earlier chapters will help to strengthen the hand, the head, and the heart. This chapter turns to the creation of new knowledge through practice-based action research and draws on all three of these qualities of professionalism to build a stronger future.

BUILDING A PROFESSIONAL FIELD ON OUR OWN KNOWLEDGE BASE

By almost any comparative standard, our field is not strong when it comes to our knowledge base, and, perhaps even more problematic, *our capacity* to build a future knowledge base through research is not strong either (Beder, 1991; Quigley, 1997). To build a profession and truly enhance professional pride inside and outside of this field, we need the heart and the hand to stay strong, but to address the complex issues we face in the 21st century—including many of the political and public image issues we continue to encounter—we need an increased capacity and enhanced ability to build upon our own knowledge in systematic, credible, and acceptable ways.

THE NEED FOR INCREASED RESEARCH CAPACITY AND RESEARCH CREDIBILITY

In recent years, governmental and other sponsors of adult literacy in various countries have been raising the accountability issue (Demetrion, 2005; Foster, 1990; Merrifield, 1998). Although it has taken various forms in various nations, developments from several federal, state and provincial government sponsors, including those in the United Kingdom, Australia, New Zealand, Canada, and the United States, have been raising the bar on accountability. As part of larger accountability issues, in the United States and other nations there is a growing demand for improved educational programming and improved instruction using more systematic research methodologies. For instance, Whitehurst with the U.S. Department of Education's Institute of Education Sciences has called for "the integration of professional wisdom with the best empirical evidence in making decisions about how to deliver instruction" (cited in Comings, 2003, p. 2). This growing demand for "evidence-based research" in ABE and literacy has, in turn, led some policy makers to urge literacy and ABE programmers to make better use of quantitative research methodologies such as experimental, quasi-experimental, and correlational methods with and without statistical controls, and case studies. Following the partnering model of the National Center for the Study of Adult Literacy and Learning (NCSALL), located at Harvard University, Comings (2003) and others have suggested that adult literacy programs might partner with expert researchers or expert research teams to conduct such quantitative research.

This recent call for "the best empirical evidence" is an important challenge for our field—one that can be met through a variety of research approaches and strategies. In addition to using quantitative methodologies, such as those recommended above which may necessitate collaboration with expert researchers, the other widely accepted approach to research is found in qualitative—sometimes called naturalistic—research. In adult literacy and basic education there is a growing international movement to build evidence-based knowledge using qualitative research. This is in cooperation with established researchers in some cases and by practitioners themselves in others.

While it is beyond the scope of this guide to discuss the merits and limitations of qualitative vs. quantitative research paradigms or review the past two to three decades of (sometimes heated) debate around the issues of which research paradigms are the most "credible" (see Gage, 1989) or most "rigorous" (see Smith & Heshusius, 1986), the social sciences provide the academic home for the disciplines of education and adult education, and the clear shift in the social sciences research has been toward qualitative research over the past few decades. This point is revisited later as the ever-contested question of credibility of research is discussed, but it is worth saying at this point that most of mainstream adult education discourse has moved beyond binary questions of "which is the best research paradigm, qualitative or quantitative?" Few academics or researchers in the adult education still argue over "best methodology" but would say, instead, we are well past that point. As Merriam has concluded, "The debate in the current literature is . . . about the extent to *which research methods* [emphasis added] characteristic of particular paradigms can or should be mixed or matched" (1991, p. 60; Firestone, 1987). Therefore, it is appropriate to consider how qualitative research, in addition to quantitative research, can be utilized to fulfill at least some of the research needs of our field (Vidich & Lyman, 2000) and explore the role adult basic education and literacy practitioners can play in creating credible knowledge and building research capacity.

Importantly, today's academic adult education researchers would widely agree that research is more a process than choices from a "tool kit." It is a way of seeing and exploring. Merriam's statement that research "should be seen as an integral part of our practice as adult educators" (1991, p. 61) is indicative of how the entire area of research has grown in adult education and literacy discourse. It is refreshing to see how many researchers have actually been working to "demystifying" research and make it part of literacy practice (e.g., Crowther, Hamilton, & Tett, 2001; Lytle & Cochran-Smith, 1990). We now see the emerging title of "practitioner-researcher" (Jarvis, 1999)—meaning practitioners who conduct and advocate for research within their own practice. We also see rising recognition and funding support for practice-based research in several countries (e.g., Campbell & Burnaby, 2001; Kemmis, 1990; Norton & Malicky, 2000; Quigley & Kuhne, 1997).

As the debates in academic and governmental circles have raged on about "Which is the best paradigm?" adult literacy practitioners have simply been building a research-in-practice movement from within their own classrooms and tutoring settings using methods such as action research, participatory research, practitioner inquiry, narrative inquiry, and case study, among others. And importantly, they have been doing so with the welcome support of state, provincial, and federal governments in the United States, Canada, Australia, and the United Kingdom, to cite but a few examples (Quigley & Norton, 2002; Rose, 2001).

If research is to be integrated with professional wisdom, as the U.S. Department of Education's Institute of Education Sciences has recommended, we continue to need:

- *An expanded capacity* for practitioners to learn about and engage in research-in-practice as part of their everyday teaching. Research should not be the exclusive domain of academics, research consultants, or government officials.
- *An improved understanding* of how the findings of such research can be confirmed as trustworthy so the findings can have dependability (or "reliability" as termed in quantitative research) across many similar settings.
- *A more comprehensive means to communicate and synthesize* what we have learned from research-in-practice, from universities, and from other institutional research settings in order to adopt, adapt, and learn more effectively across North America and around the globe.

Each of these needs is addressed in this chapter, including a "hands on" discussion of *how you can put an action research method into your daily practice.* But first, you may well be asking the most basic question: "While this is all very interesting, why should I engage in this in the first place? After all, aren't we supposed to be teachers, tutors and administrators? Isn't someone else paid to do research work?"

Why Should I Be a "Researcher?"

In Pennsylvania, Virginia, Texas, California, Kentucky, New England, and Kansas; in Canada's provinces of British Columbia, Alberta, Saskatchewan, Ontario, Nova Scotia, Newfoundland and Labrador; across Australia and England; to name but a few international initiatives, federal, state, and provincial governments have been encouraging the growth of research-in-practice networks (Quigley & Norton, 2001; and see the list of sample Websites at the end of this chapter). Although this is a piecemeal grassroots research revolution, hundreds of practitioners and learners are engaged in the movement (Belzer &

St. Clair, 2003; Burnaford, Fischer, & Hobson, 2001; Flecho, 2000). Why?

We Too Are Learners

One reason is simply that we too are adult learners. We too seek answers in order to do this complex work. Many will agree that waiting for expert researchers and consulting teams to answer everyday questions, or seeking the amounts of money typically needed to hire them, is simply unrealistic. But beyond this, as already seen, practitioners aspire to professional conduct and, for many, being able to address classroom and program issues in a systematic and trustworthy manner comes with that aspiration. Why are so many literacy practitioners coming forward to engage in professional development? As noted in Chapter 1, it is because they have the values and the motivation that sets professionals apart. The quest to do a better job simply because it is the right thing to do is surely at the very heart of vocation, of a calling, and of professionalism as originally conceived centuries ago.

As a result of the current practitioner-researcher revolution, questions about student retention, most effective teaching methods, strategies for student recruitment, ways to work with student learning disabilities, best methods within language instruction, and a host of larger and smaller questions are being investigated in ABE and literacy programs at this moment.

Even going beyond the classroom, literacy practitioner-researchers in Canada, for instance, have investigated how adults with low literacy skills go about learning *outside* the classroom and on their own (Niks, Allen, Davies, McRae, Nonesuch, 2003). They are drawing on the rich area of research and theory in the New Literacy Studies movement from the United Kingdom for better ways to understand the very nature of literacy and learning (e.g., Demetrion, 2005; Ewing, 2003). At the policy level, the research-in-practice movement is playing a role in critiquing and advising governmental policy in England (Quigley

& Norton, 2001). The research-in-practice movement is exploring issues in prison literacy, family literacy, work-place literacy,
community-based literacy (e.g., Davidson 2001; Zacharakis-
Jutz, 2001). Practitioner-researchers are seeking to resolve immediate issues that the academic community simply hasn't the
capacity to address.

Sometimes the findings of these practitioner-researchers
have been posted on Websites; sometimes they have been published in monographs or newsletters (see the Websites at the end
of this chapter). Unfortunately, most of the new practitioner-
researchers have not communicated their findings widely or
tested them sufficiently to build high levels of dependability and
trustworthiness in the findings.

In summary, practitioner-researchers are beginning to build
a stronger knowledge base on a global level. They are learning
from practice and beginning to share that learning. As Zora
Neale Hurston put it, they are "poking and prying with purpose" (1942, p. 174).

Let's take a closer look at the research method which, according to a recent survey I was involved with, is the most widely
used for research-in-practice in North American adult literacy
(Quigley & Norton, 2001). What is it and how does it work?

What Is Action Research and What Are Some of Its Limitations?

Definitions of action research differ, types of action research differ (Kemmis, 1990; Zeichner, 2001), but there is a
common understanding in the literature that, *in an action research project, we systematically analyze a problem, review the
literature and relevant experience, set a baseline for purposes
of comparative analysis, systematically gather evidence on observed change(s), and collectively reflect on the outcomes.* As the
education literature will attest, research-in-practice has also
been widely used for the development of professional development skills such as critical thinking, team building, leadership

building, and a range of attendant research skills even as it is creating knowledge (Burnaford, Fischer, & Hobson, 2001; Smith & Hofer, 2003). By following systematic steps, trustworthiness and dependability issues can be enhanced.

However, it is important to add that action research—the method among many to be discussed here—is not a panacea for literacy and ABE. For instance, action research is not usually designed to bring about radical or "deep" change in society or institutions (Zeichner, 2001). In such social change cases, participatory research—sometimes referred to as "participatory action research" in education—is what our field has typically looked to for many years (Hall, 2001; Kemmis & McTaggart, 1988; Quigley, 2005; Reason & Bradbury, 2002). As will be seen, action research is not recommended when the project has too many outside influences beyond a practitioner's control. With these qualifiers, "a better articulation and justification of the educational rationale for what goes on" (Kemmis & McTaggart, 1988, p. 5) can be offered through action research, and the evidence from action research can help us advocate for added resources and help make clear that the changes we are making in our practice are in fact effective, meaningful, and worth supporting.

USING ACTION RESEARCH IN OUR DAILY WORK

So far in this book, you have been engaged in discussions with your co-learners, keeping a learning journal, and been part of reflectivity through the earlier chapters. This is the very same process that is encouraged for action research. With this chapter, you should be in a strong position to take on an action research study. In the model to be described, it is strongly suggested that the problem you choose and the study you undertake should be conducted with the help of research friends. These may be your co-learners, but the nature of the project is somewhat different from what we have done so far, so there may be others interested in the same questions as you are who are also knowledgeable about these issues and able to give some advice and input as you go along (Argyris, Putnam, & McLain Smith, 1985; Cochran-Smith & Lytle, 1993; Smith & Hofer, 2002; Quigley & Norton, 2002). Just as it was recommended you don't learn alone in this guide, it is recommended you try not to research alone. Both the study and you will be the better for it if you have a group to assist and advise you.

A lot of information is covered in the next "hands-on" section. A checklist is provided at chapter end to help you with projects into the future.

THE FOUR MAIN PHASES OF ACTION RESEARCH

From Kurt Lewin, who is often credited with establishing the action research method, to Stephen Cory, often recognized as having popularized the method in U.S. schools, to more recent advocates for this method in university teacher education programs (e.g., Cochran-Smith & Lytle, 1993), to advocates for its acceptance in adult education academic settings (e.g., Quigley & Watkins, 2001), four phases can be found in each of the iterations of what goes into the action research process:

1. Problem-Posing

2. Planning

3. Observing

4. Reflecting

These four phases create a complete cycle. At the end of the fourth stage—the reflection stage—you might decide to try yet another full cycle that approaches the same issue from a somewhat new direction guided by what you have learned so far. Action research doesn't exactly "end." It often leads to multiple cycles of problem-posing and problem solving that can enable the adult educator, the program, and the entire institution—if not the entire region or wider community—to successfully address challenging issues on deeper and deeper levels over

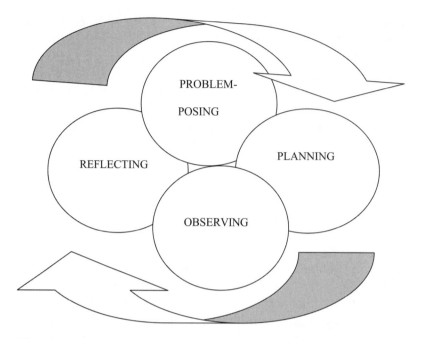

Figure 5.1 The Four Main Phases of Action research

time. A fictitious example will be given here to help make this clear, but the figure shown below on the four phases may help as well.

Let's now look at the first phase of an action research project and do so with a problem that faces so many literacy and ABE teachers today. I would have chosen the high-priority issue of student attrition for the example used, but I have discussed that topic elsewhere using the action research approach (Quigley, 1997; Quigley, 1998). Instead, since it is the method and not the problem that matters here, the example I have chosen (at the suggestion of some practitioners) is the problem of age difference in the classroom. Again, this may not be *your problem*, but the systematic process effectively stays consistent in all action research studies. So I hope this discussion will give you a working example to discuss with your research co-learners.

" 'The Itch': How Can I Teach Younger and More Mature Adults Together?" Let's take a fictitious example of teaching a "mixed-age group." Judy has a classroom of 20 ABE students in a center for ABE and literacy. Her current class is mostly made up of adults between 17 and 21 years of age. But, there are two adults in Judy's class who are in their late 50s, Walter and Phyllis. This older pair seems to slow the class down. They need to have things explained more than once. They can't always hear what is being said, they almost always miss the jokes and innuendos, and they just don't "get" the slang and jokes used by the younger students. Worse, the two older students just ask too many questions. Walter and Phyllis are obviously "different" in this context. When they try to tell their stories and, at times, begin a statement with: "When I was your age . . . ," eyes roll. Students groan. Walter is becoming visibly frustrated, and his attendance is beginning to drop off. Phyllis is becoming more silent. It seems the situation is only getting worse, no matter what Judy tries. Here's an "itch" for a study.

PHASE ONE: PROBLEM-POSING

The "Itch": Action research typically begins with an "itch" (Quigley & Kuhne, 1997). You know something isn't working as well as it should in daily practice. You find yourself asking: "How can I fix this?" Time is being wasted in trying to address the same issue over and over. In the case at hand, Walter and Phyllis are being made to feel irrelevant, and Walter is talking about quitting. The same age-mix problem is occurring in other classrooms as well. This fictitious scenario could have been the reverse scenario with a younger group being "isolated" in the midst of a majority of more mature learners. Nothing we try is working.

Creating a Research Circle: Perhaps the most difficult step for an adult education volunteer, teacher, program planner, administrator, counselor, or policy maker in the action research process is to get a solid grasp on the *actual problem*. We are too quick to jump to "solutions" before asking the right questions. So first try to identify the "researchable question." You will probably find that, just when we think we have found "the problem," you remove another layer of the onion and there's another related problem right below it. This is why it is so important to have knowledgeable friends to assist you in the problem-posing stage. Create a group of research co-learners who will be meeting with you. Face-to-face is best, but phone and e-mail can work too. This is your research circle. Here are your advisors, your helpers, and your support group. They may also be the beneficiaries of the study outcomes as well.

This will be a problem-solving group, somewhat different from the co-learners seen in previous chapters. As noted, the new circle *may* comprise many of the same people as those in your learning circle, but the research co-learners will be discussing a single problem, reflecting on ways to deal with it, reflecting on the data, and deciding with you if a second cycle makes sense. They will be walking 360 degrees around the issue with you.

"Who Can I Talk With About This?" In this case of Walter and Phyllis, Judy first brings four other teachers together to create a research circle. Each has ABE experience and two are currently experiencing the same problem. Together they consider, "What do our various situations have in common? How do they differ? What actions, comments, or classroom topics seem to trigger these in-classroom tensions? Is there anything about seating patterns, timetables, times of the day, or days of the week that are involved in this? Are we dealing with only one or two "young leaders" whom a few others are following? What part do we, the teachers, play in perhaps enabling this dynamic?" The group meets more than once to talk about the dynamics and the patterns of the involved.

Toward a Positive Intervention: Having a research circle explore the problems involved and deciding what is changeable—that is, what part of the problem can be influenced and managed—is vital. Consider what has been tried in the various classrooms over time and what approach seemed to make a difference in those cases. Brainstorm these and other ideas that may address the problem. Use a flip chart or blackboard to jot them down. Then from these make a short list of the group's "best hunches" regarding the aspect of the problem you think you are able to address at this time. But before deciding on your best hunch and concluding this stage of the project, take some time to search the literature using the Internet (see the listing of Websites at the end of this chapter) and try searching databases at a library such as the ERIC database. Armed with information, try to decide on the intervention you will use. But before a final decision, ask: "Have our discussions and searches for other studies altered the problem as was initially perceived and defined? Are we still on the same initial "itch?""

To make your choice of the best intervention, you can put your "best hunches" on a flip chart. It is a good idea to save the top three or four alternative possibilities if the one you now have chosen isn't practical for some reason. One more thing, consider what barriers might make the selected intervention fail. How could those barriers be overcome if they arise?

"What Can We Try to Help Walter and Phyllis? What Are Our Best Hunches?" Judy's research circle had a lot of good ideas, such as: 1) "What about moving Walter and Phyllis to another classroom and just keep ages separated in future? Maybe our center needs age-based classrooms." 2) "How about making this a classroom discussion topic in Judy's classroom? Why not have Walter and Phyllis involved in it?" 3) "Why not just take the 'young leaders' aside and talk with them alone about how they are behaving and ask them to change? The centre director can do it if Judy doesn't want to. If they don't shape up, drop them from the program." 4) "We could take Walter and Phyllis aside and ask them for their suggestions; it's their lives, after all." 5) "How about a way that Walter and Phyllis can be respected on their own terms? Maybe having them mentor others in the classroom." Each hunch has potential, but which is the best hunch? Which to try? Before deciding, each of the members of the research circle got involved in a literature search. Judy went to the local library, since she knows the reference librarian and would

ask for help searching ERIC, ProQuest, and any other major adult education databases. Two others would search the Websites at the end of this chapter. The other two would talk with the other teachers and contact some other programs to see what they do in these cases.

Conducting a Literature Search on the Question. As seen in the example, before arriving at the best hunch intervention, see what research already exists on this topic and try to find out what others have done in literacy practice to handle this very situation. There's nothing new under the sun, as they say. In this important step, the challenge is to find out what others have learned through systematic inquiry and see what can be applied to your situation.

Maybe We Should Put a Special Task Force Together. Having the context, other research, and others' experience, and as much background as possible at this point, and having discussed and brainstormed possible interventions down to a short list and even a best hunch, may not be enough. Often you are ready to start, but sometimes there are just too many good intervention ideas and you can't decide which hunch is best. If this happens, rather than plunging ahead, you probably need a longer problem-posing period involving more expertise. In this case, consider adding those with special expertise to your research circle (Fetterman, 1997). It could include learners, it could include community people, it could include counselors, or reading specialists, medical people, social workers, community leaders, or more practitioners from other programs.

"A Task Force That Changed Practice Across a State." The fictitious example of Walter and Phyllis here is not as suitable to make this point as one where I personally worked with a group of literacy/ABE teachers and administrators in Pennsylvania. One literacy coordinator was struggling with how to encourage her rural literacy tutors, spread over a huge geographic area, to send their time sheets back. They were due every Friday. These

time sheets, while a nuisance perhaps, were the reported hours each tutor volunteered each week, and the completed forms were necessary to fund the project. No time sheets, no grant. We brainstormed and came up with more than 40 best hunches. These included: 1) "Encourage the rural tutors with incentives like prizes, such as pizza coupons"; 2) "Use phone trees to remind tutors at week's end to fill them in and send them"; 3) "Just 'fire' those tutors who don't follow the requirements"; 4) "Have administrative assistants travel the region and drop in," and on and on. We didn't know which hunch was best or what to try. We realized we were actually spending time speculating on what the problems really were. A literature search was of no help on this one, so we agreed that, at the annual tutors' meeting, a volunteer task force of about five tutors would be struck to review our short list of suggestions. Surprisingly, to me at least, that small group later came up with a hunch we hadn't considered at all. It changed the institutional procedures and policies of that college—and others—across the state. "Simply have the tutored students fill out the forms *with their tutor* every Friday." The time sheet became a statement of progress the learners looked forward to. Instead of nuisance paper work, here was a point of attendance discussion for the tutor, a week-end "reward," and a teaching tool for writing and numeracy. The problem was solved. The outcomes have been adopted across the state, and I was reminded to trust the expertise of teachers and learners.

But Maybe We Shouldn't Use Action Research at All. Action research, as noted, is not a panacea and may *not* be the best approach to study a problem. Once you begin to uncover the layers of the issues involved, your research co-learners may decide the problems are so emotionally charged, or so personality-based, or so politically driven, or have so many outside mitigating factors and uncertainties that are beyond your control that an action research intervention just can't work here. Personal difficulties on the job with a supervisor is one example. Students in class who are court-ordered to be there and sit angrily waiting to "escape" may be another. Faltering funding from a grantor can be another. Some practice-based problems simply require other actions or other research approaches. These approaches may need to be longitudinal in nature; or wider than an local action research project to draw a large sample of participants; or may require a wide-scale experimental study; or just may need political action (Fernandes & Tandon, 1981; Merriam & Simpson, 2000). Only enter an action research project if it seems to fit the question, not the other way round.

Think Small. One of the biggest pitfalls of action research projects is the desire to try to change too much, too soon. Due to on-the-job pressures, we often get into a mode of being "too busy to think." We "produce," "we fix," we move things along and can find ourselves plunging ahead before asking the right questions or taking on more than we can possibly study in one action research cycle. In general, undertake only what you can manage and build your answers step-by-step through small, well understood cycles of action research. As a rule of thumb, only when you can write the question to be studied in a single interrogative sentence are you ready to begin. Before deciding on the best hunch, be able to state the actual question. Even if the research circle decides to modify it along the way—which can be done with action research—the precise question needs to be clear.

"Okay. Here's Our Intervention for the Walter/Phyllis Study": There were many options. After discussing each one, it was decided the best hunch from the short list was to set up a mentoring-partner approach. Walter is a good reader and writer. Phyllis excels in math. Maybe mentoring will help individualize the group—that is, break down the group. Maybe it will give Walter and Phyllis a chance to show their own mature skills and knowledge.

However, on further discussion, Judy pointed out that singling out *only* Walter and Phyllis as mentors and letting them gain respect for their knowledge and skills will make them very self-conscious. It might even make a bad situation worse. The research co-learners decided to continue building on the interdependent learning model intake discussed in Chapter 4 by setting up a partner-mentoring relationship between pairs of learners throughout the classroom. Walter will work with Bruce, one of the most outspoken of the younger learners, but one who is very concerned with grades. Bruce struggles with reading so that should be a good match. Phyllis will be paired with Cindy, who is having trouble with math and is very conscientious. Likewise, all other students in the class will be partnered with a mentor during the subject periods of reading and math. Judy will explain that partners can be changed upon request. If others are willing to switch, that is.

So they had the intervention but then someone asked, "What is it we are really going to be looking for here? Is it the effectiveness of mentoring in a classroom? Maybe we should be seeing if it helps with grades overall. What was the original question anyway?" Judy reminded everyone she just wanted Walter and Phyllis to fit in better, adding: "Now I've got this big project on my hands." The others agreed they would help her since mentoring just might be something everyone could use. So the discussion focused on the question: "How will we know success if and when we see it? What are we actually going to measure here?"

Naming the Benchmark: We now have the question and we look forward to improving the situation with an intervention, but we now need to ask: "What are we really studying and, to know if we have succeeded, what are we comparing it to?" A clear question and a benchmark are often needed in order to be able to say, "It once was like this, and now it's like this. Here are the demonstrable changes and the evidence." We need to decide what the patterns of behaviors, or attitudes, or levels of knowing were *initially* and, through numerical or narrative data collection techniques, *how they have changed*. What's different, and compared to what?

It is important to have a benchmark that will give a reliable comparison. For instance, if we look for attendance rate improvements, we will typically measure against attendance before the intervention. But probably comparing the outcomes with attendance records *over the same time period last year,* or using the past three years, or more if possible, will really allow for variations in the seasonal time period. The pre-Christmas period may not be "typical," but the last three pre-Christmas periods can give us a benchmark to measure this period against. So this involves accessing the records for the program including the grades. We will need a grades benchmark for a comparison point if we are seeking to study improvement in grade levels. Even attitudes can be compared, if we have a benchmark, by asking, "What were attitudes, even levels of satisfaction, before the intervention? What are they like afterward?" Using good, consistent data collection techniques is the essence of a successful action research study.

"Okay, Here's Our Questions and Benchmarks for the Study:" The group was concerned about dependability and trustworthiness of the findings if they were going to try the mentoring approach in other classrooms later. After all, "It may work for Judy's class, but I don't have Walter and Phyllis. Mine are a different problem. Why try this later unless there's a good reason to think mentoring will transfer for my age-mix problems?" The group considered having two or three other teachers who were having the same age-mix problem try the same intervention at the same time, and then compare the outcomes of all three. That would enhance credibility of the findings. They thought about having Judy repeat the study later in her classroom in the spring with a new group of learners to build confidence in the findings. The others could try it in the fall. But for right now, the research co-learners wrote this question: "Will creating a mentor-partnership between two older students with two younger students on math and reading lead to greater acceptance of the two older learners in the class? We will reasonably assume it does if there is an increase in the acceptance of the two older students by the others. Judy will keep a journal and observe changes, and there will be an exit interview for Walter and Phyllis and whomever Judy pairs with them."

When Judy brought up the fact that making Walter and Phyllis the center of the study will make them self-conscious, the exact question became refined to: "If all the students in Judy's ABE classroom are in paired mentoring partnerships around reading and math, will: 1) the partnership between Cindy and Phyllis, and Bruce and Walter, respectively, lead to full acceptance of Phyllis and Walter by the other students?" This will be measured by the attitudes and acceptance of Phyllis and Walter *prior* to and *after* trying this intervention."

But then they saw some other possibilities here. If Judy was going to this much effort, why not add some secondary questions: 1) "Will Walter's and Phyllis's *attendance rates* improve and will overall *attendance rates* improve? We will know both by comparing Phyllis's and Walter's attendance before and after the intervention, and the class's attendance rates by going back 3 years in the same seasonal period. 2) Will overall *class grades* improve when we compare the trial period with the class grades for the last three years in the same seasonal months? But since past student evaluation feedback records were kept by Judy, why not add another? 3) Will student satisfaction improve during the trial period, as compared with the satisfaction rates as collected by this teacher?

It's an ambitious project, but everyone across the whole ABE program is excited and interested to see if mentoring will lead to major improvements across the entire centre.

PHASE TWO: PLANNING THE ACTION RESEARCH PROJECT

We have made all the major decisions. We have a question, or more than one, that we know we can manage. We have a way to compare progress with benchmarks. Now for the details to make the project go. Typically, there are at least six organizing questions that need to be answered in this planning stage:

1) When should we begin the project and when should we stop? **The timeline**

2) How will we inform or involve those in the project? **The informed consent**

3) What administrative approvals will we need? **The institutional approvals**

4) What other resources or preparations will be needed? **Resources**

5) How can we collect data? **The data collection techniques**

6) What are our "indicators of success?" **The criteria for success**

"Here's Our Plan for Walter and Phyllis": For the timeline, the study will begin next Monday if the teacher can get the approval from her supervisor at the ABE Center. Judy will ask her students this Friday if they will try pairs mentoring in reading and math to see if it improves attendance, grades, and overall student satisfaction. If some say no, they will be told it's okay and they don't have to but the project will still go ahead. The project will last three months. Students can change their minds and stop participating just by indicating this to the teacher. Also, it will be explained: "A pair can switch if there is another pair that wants to change. Each student will be paired with another based on individual knowledge and progress in math and reading. Those ahead of the others in the individualized program will sit with their partner and help with questions as needed. And more problem-solving questions will be used by the pairs. Anyone can suggest them. Real-life experiences in math and reading are welcome."

As for success criteria, if Judy observes greater acceptance of Walter and Phyllis by a decrease in negative comments toward them and an increase in behaviors showing the same respect toward Walter and Phyllis as any other student, then the study will meet this success criterion. She'll keep field notes (see chapter end) and her own learning journal. For the other secondary questions, if there is a 10% improvement in attendance overall, and a 10% improvement in Walter's and Phyllis's too, and a minimum of a 5% improvement in grade levels for math and reading, then the secondary success criteria will have been met as well. Someone pointed out that dropout rates will be easy to follow as well if the attendance is already being compared. So retention and a minimum of 10% increase over the past 3 years was added.

If it is decided to go to a second cycle, a more refined question, new success criteria, and a new timeline will be needed, as well as new approvals and consents. But before discussing the outcomes or their dependability and trustworthiness, let's first look at just how data—or evidence—can be collected in the observing stage.

PHASE THREE: THE OBSERVING PHASE

Once the study is put into motion, it is time to see what will happen and collect evidence. Since this is action research, there is always room for change in the design and the data collection methods. Action research understands that situations in the lives of adults and institutions change. No classroom or tutoring situation is frozen in time waiting to be observed. As situations arise, the research circle can make adjustments.

How Can We Collect Evidence? More than one technique for collecting data will help us know if the project is actually making a difference. The use of several data collection methods is called "triangulation" of evidence. It makes studies more meaningful and strengthens applicability to other classrooms. As a rule of thumb, having *at least* three data collection techniques, resulting in at least three data sets, is recommended. They allow for overlapping data that point to the same conclusions through triangulation of the data. Some of the standard ways to collect data are listed and briefly described at the end of this chapter, but a few of the more common ones for action research are seen next in our case study.

"Here's How We'll Collect Data in the Walter and Phyllis Study: In the Walter and Phyllis study, Judy will keep in-class field notes and a research journal with regular entries, reflecting on what is occurring in the classroom during the study. It is also decided that all the students will keep learning journals too and discuss their reflections regularly in class. Do they like this mentoring idea? Is it helping? Why or why not? Each student will have an exit interview with a member of the original intake team (not

the classroom teacher, to minimize the chance that the learners may not say what they actually think to the classroom teacher). This will be compared using the evaluation records and exit interview data from 3 previous years that Judy kept. If any drop out, they will try to be reached by a member of the intake team for a telephone exit or, better, a face-to-face interview. Dropout rates will be compared with the records of the previous 3 years.

This is all a fair amount of work. Happily, Judy's research co-learners decided they would do the front office records analysis and conduct the exit interviews.

Having run the project, it is time for the reflection stage. Was it worth all the planning and work?

PHASE FOUR: THE REFLECTION PHASE

When the timeline is reached, reassemble the research circle and reflect on the data.

So, What Have We Learned? The research circle should help the teacher go through the collected data and compare them to the benchmarks. It should be done systematically so trustworthiness of the results is maintained. The review can be conducted with some in the research circle taking certain data sets (such as in the Walter-Phyllis case, two from the circle taking the student journals and two taking the teacher journals) and others studying other data (such as comparing the records on grades, attendance, and dropout). They can then reverse roles to see if everyone reaches the same *independent* conclusions looking at the same data. Or, although it's more time consuming, each member can individually examine all the data sets and come back together as a group to see if everyone is agreed that the same conclusions have been reached. The idea here is to have checks so there is independent agreement on patterns and changes observed.

One question is vital: "Did the outcomes meet the criteria for success?" If they did, then the second question should be: "Should a second cycle now take place?" Before moving on, ask:

"Can we do this again in another classroom, besides repeating it in the same classroom?" Remember, there can be many reasons for the findings seen. The same intervention may lead to quite different results if tried with a new group of students. But if the research circle finds that the criteria for success aren't met on some or all of the questions, they may decide that the intervention was the wrong hunch and it is not worth pursuing or recommending further study. "We tried, we failed — but we know more than when we began. Every teacher has benefited to this extent."

However, if the research circle finds that an intervention meets the criteria, or has partially succeeded and there is *sufficient promise* at this point to carry on, the teachers in the program should attempt another cycle before adopting this approach for the future. We need a second run to build confidence in what we found. We always need to answer the bottom-line critique: "How trustworthy and consistent are the findings? When are we ready to adopt this approach in other classrooms or programs and put it on our Website? When can we reasonably assume that this intervention was the reason for the change?"

So, to build dependability and trustworthiness, the same study should be conducted again in the same or another classroom or center on another occasion. If the outcomes meet the criteria for success over and over, you will have enhanced the strength of the findings. If this study is run concurrently in two classrooms or centers with the same results, trustworthiness and dependability are enhanced once again. Being able to repeat the outcomes is a solid sign that you have found a better way. Questions of trustworthiness and dependability diminish with each successful run of the project.

"It Was a Complete Success—Almost—in the Walter and Phyllis Study:" This study lasted 3 months. The results on acceptance of our two older learners were compared with the 2 months before the intervention. The teacher's research journal, the students' journals, and the exit interviews were compared with 3 previous years' records. This triangulation of these three data sets told the research circle that the approach was a success with respect to

acceptance. Attitudes and behaviors changed. Walter and Phyllis went on to do extremely well in the program, and graduated. Secondly, the data collected during the study compared with the period before the study showed that Walter's and Phyllis's attendance improved. When the overall attendance during the trial period was compared with the same time period over the previous 3 years, overall attendance went up by a full 13%. The mentoring hunch also improved overall satisfaction with the program when the exit interviews were compared with previous years' exit interviews and when the students' journals were reviewed. Likewise, the teacher's journal showed that she thought the class atmosphere improved and she was far happier with the conduct of learners with partnering. But it was not all good news. The grades did not improve 5% for the entire class. Perhaps we were asking too much of the project?

It was decided to re-test the age-mix study with this same set of "acceptance" interventions in two other classrooms that had a similar age-mix problem, but the idea of partnering for classwide grade improvement needed more thought. Then one of the research circle teachers noticed that math skills did improve rapidly for Cindy and for a few others. "Why not try partners in math, and only math, in my classroom as a spin-off study? Test for one thing only. Mentoring for math. Nothing else." So here was a new direction for the study. Maybe partnerships could improve math skills if studied in pairs.

WHERE TO FROM HERE? THE WIDENING VALUE OF ACTION RESEARCH

Whatever the outcomes and decisions at the end of each cycle, you can be assured that others in the literacy community will want to know the results. "What did you learn that I can try?" is the common question at literacy and ABE conferences and workshops. Always try to communicate what you found—no matter if you met your criteria or simply gave up on the project mid-way or feel your efforts were "inadequate." You tried and you learned more than others facing the same prob-

lem. You set an example for critical thinking and reflective practice for others. Trying has more value than we often think.

The Importance of Reaching Out. Ours is really a field of endless "wheel re-invention." On an international level, we have
very similar problems within very similar forms of curricula
with very similar teaching goals. Ultimately, not wanting to
overgeneralize, or oversimplify, similar learners come into programs across North America and beyond. When compared to
some areas of mainstream adult education, such as international
corporate training or adult self-directed learning, ours is won-
derfully consistent. In literacy and adult basic education, what
we learn will be of help to someone else in our field.

If we can just enhance the dependability and trustworthiness of our research findings, if we can just share them on Websites or in professional journals, in newsletters and at conferences, then we will have moved the entire region, or state/
province, or international field ahead. And we can take increasing personal pride in knowing we are drawing from—and contributing to—evidence-based knowledge from within our own
practice.

BUT IS ACTION RESEARCH REALLY VALID AND RELIABLE?

This chapter began by indicating that there have been
"research-paradigm wars" for many years in the academic community. This point may be of more interest to those in the academic community than in literacy practice. However, asking if
action research is "valid and reliable" is included at the end of
this chapter since some practitioners, researchers, and program
funding agencies will not be persuaded that action research is
"good research" without such answers. Of course, there are
those who will dismiss all qualitative methods just in principle,
believing *only* empirical, quantitative experimental research resulting from statistical, controlled experimental methodologies
can produce the evidence necessary for true validity and reli-

ability. Anything "less" won't have generalizability, therefore isn't really research at all. The more typical view in the social sciences adult education is much more accepting of qualitative methods.

Yet there has been criticism of action research from within the adult education research community itself. In 1984, Merriam and Simpson argued that action research "can only make minimal contributions to the body of knowledge in any field of study" (2000, p. 108) because "it lacks external and internal controls" (p. 108). It can only have "little generalizability" (p. 108). They revised this stance somewhat in 1995 and again in 2000 (using the same wording which actually appears on the very same page of both editions), saying, "action research . . . has its limitations. Because it lacks external and internal controls, generalizability of results are limited to the specific circumstances and conditions in which the research was done" (p. 125).

Since action research is the method used most by literacy practitioners in the international research-in-practice movement (Quigley & Norton, 2002), and since the validity/reliability question is sometimes raised by sponsors and researchers, this critique is worth discussing here.

The noted researchers Guba and Lincoln say the "consistency of studies is an empirical matter" (1988, p. 121). Consistency, clearly, is a key aspect of this discussion. How can consistency—and trustworthiness of the findings of action research—be enhanced and ultimately assured? One common approach across all qualitative research is to use "overlap" (p. 121), another term for what was here called "repeated cycles." Put simply, if the "results from two or more different approaches" (p. 121) can show consistent patterns, "the imperfections of one are canceled or covered up by the strengths of a second" (p. 121). Therefore, by repeated cycles in qualitative research, including action research, we can build consistency and trustworthiness. The confidence in the outcomes increases. How can we do this in our classrooms? Since action research has such a wonderful capacity for flexibility, it can be conducted in the same setting or same classroom several times, or it can be applied in several settings or classrooms with multiple groups of learners to address the same issue, always through repeated cycles. This all builds trustworthiness and consistency in the evidence, ultimately to the point of "saturation" when the outcomes are essentially the same every time. The results are consistent. They are also trustworthy because they come out the same time over time.

A second response to any critique of consistency and trustworthiness is to apply "stepwise replication" (Guba & Lincoln, 1988, p. 121). This rather intimidating term is basically the "concurrency" seen earlier where a study group can be divided into two random halves. If the same results occur in the same classroom, or in two similar classrooms, or two locations *concurrently*, consistency and trustworthiness again increase (pp. 123–124). The teachers can cross-check for "major patterns and important nuances" (Patton, 1987, p. 24), and if the triangulation of concurrent data in more than one setting points to the same set of conclusions, trustworthiness and consistency are again enhanced.

Ironically, these very approaches used in qualitative research can be found within the quantitative school itself. The famous experimental researcher, Lee Cronbach, (1980) argued in favor of the approaches seen here both for qualitative and quantitative research. He actually argued against experimental designs in some instances saying they can become so narrowly focused and controlled that studies can basically become irrelevant beyond their own controlled circumstances. Cronbach argued for "extrapolation" (1980, pp. 231–235) as the way to enhance validity and credibility in research. Michael Q. Patton also agreed that extrapolation of consistent findings from multiple-setting evidence—what is called triangulation in this chapter—can allow for "modest speculations on the likely applications of findings to other situations under similar, but not identical, conditions" (1987, p. 168). This extrapolation approach, according to Cronbach, can be highly useful if it is "logical, thoughtful, and problem-oriented rather than statistical and probalistic" (1980, p. 168). Therefore, if we can extrapolate findings that are consistent, the trustworthiness and dependability—or "validity" and "reliability" to use the terms of the quantitative school—for action research should be acceptable for "modest speculation" among even the harshest of our critics. But we can go even further than this.

To build consistency even further we can also employ an "audit trail" (Guba & Lincoln, 1988, p. 122). Here is another impressive term that simply means if the way that the evidence was collected and analyzed for the conclusions "can be audited by a second investigator or team," then it can be safely said that "substantively and methodologically sound options were chosen" (p. 122). Put succinctly, "Just as General Electric must turn to Price, Waterhouse if the audit of its books is to have any credibility" (pp. 122–123), so can we have a clear audit trail to enhance confidence in the evidence we have collected. This third enhancement is easily done in action research and was seen in the discussion earlier during the reflection stage when the research co-learners conducted an independent analysis of the data using cross-checks. These final steps can once again take us a long way to meeting the goal of trustworthiness and consistency (Quigley & Kuhne, 1997). Doubts about the generalizability of action research can be alleviated in adult literacy education using action research if we take these kinds of steps with these standard techniques.

What this all adds up to is, if we apply the integration of professional wisdom to dependable and trustworthy research in literacy education, then we can surely meet any reasonable expectation on "how to deliver instruction," as Whitehurst (cited in Comings, 2003, p. 2) has encouraged practitioners to do.

Again, action research is not the panacea for all literacy practice, research or credibility issues. There are other qualitative and quantitiative methods being used to good effect in literacy, and we can make better use of institute, consultant, and university-based research, much of which is accessible on Internet Websites and published in journals and books, as noted at the end of this chapter. But rather than be "practice apologists" or "passive recipients of received research," we have the means to contribute to knowledge. We can go beyond the "specific circumstances and conditions in which the research was done," as Merriam and Simpson put it, and we can be part of a movement where "the teacher is also the researcher who can generate knowledge about his or her practice (2000, p. 123). Adult literacy researcher-practitioners are building a stronger research capacity for the future, but I think we need to work on a larger canvas, as seen next.

A PROPOSAL FOR INTERDEPENDENT LEARNING ACROSS OUR FIELD

I think of how many times I have been at energy-charged tables in so many states and provinces when teachers, tutors, and administrators are working collaboratively through a research-in-practice problem. Pizza boxes on the table, flip chart pages taped to the walls, the room alive with talk and laughter. So much is learned and shared in such collaborative settings that I am acutely aware that no book—including this one—can ever match it. Wouldn't it be wonderful *if more programs* worked on problems collaboratively using research-in-practice methodologies as part of their practice? If only more were working toward enhancing the trustworthiness and dependability of their evidence-based research, and being acknowledged for it by policy makers, sponsors, and other researchers outside of literacy. Wouldn't it be great if Websites with project problems, project descriptions, and findings were posted along with a contact person to communicate for details? Imagine practitioners struggling, then communicating with other researcher-practitioners in countries around the world on the Internet about recruitment, retention, teaching methods, evaluation, learning styles, mixed age groups, and a host of other problems. Across ESL, family literacy, corrections literacy, workplace literacy, and so many other literacy areas, we would not have to re-discover essentially the same problems over and over and re-invent the same wheel at thousands of sites.

Imagine if the vast majority of practitioners—with their learners in many cases—could just go to the Internet knowing they could find postings on practical, usable, trustworthy, consistent research outcomes—including research from universities, literacy institutes, and consultants—and then adapt, adopt, or re-test the most appropriate findings and methods. And do so in dialogue with those who posted it. Imagine the power of simply being able to use what others have found in practice, including from university and other settings, by simply using the Internet and local literature searches. What a breakthrough it would be if we had an interdependent field of practice across an international community of teacher-researcher colleagues (Quigley, 2001).

"FIRST WE MUST DREAM;
NOTHING IS HARDER"

John Lennon once said, "Maybe I'm a dreamer, but I'm not the only one. . . . " What if more Websites not only had current research problems, descriptions, and outcomes of their projects posted but also details on where and when adult literacy research training workshops, courses, and institutes were available? What if more of these training workshops were on-line? In fact, the beginning of such "research-coordination" is developing at the Canadian *Literacies* journal Website (www. literacyjournal.ca). To dream even more, imagine if research-in-practice studies were not piecemeal but gave us problem-solving strategies for a whole region, state, province or across a community, all the while seeking to enhance consistency and trustworthiness of the findings. In the late 1990s, a large number of Kentucky literacy practitioners set out to address the single, common issue of retention in literacy through action research with the support of their state government. Imagine how helpful it would be if local findings as well as relevant literature as usually found in print-based and electronic journals were posted together. Any practitioner in any setting with internet could learn from collected "literature searches." They could communicate directly with one another on what they had done. Imagine if we not only advocated interdependence in the classroom but also for our own learning using a larger canvas.

If we could just get past regional and national parochialisms

—often encouraged by chauvinistic funding policy restrictions—
we may one day see a central, internationally linked clearing-
house for adult literacy research that not only compiles and co-
ordinates literacy research but also synthesizes what is known
to be trustworthy and consistent from practitioner-researchers
and academic researchers on multiple relevant topics. One-stop
research sites for common practice problems.

If only the learned *skills of our hand* and the *knowledge
from our collective heads* would be better shared. In addition to
research-in-practice, if only *stories from the heart* about us and
by us, about our learners and by our learners were available for
the world to see. Imagine how all of this would encourage and
inspire other practitioners and learners working in isolation.
Perhaps this guide will help move us closer to this dream—
toward a prouder, more respected professional field working in
closer harmony world-wide. Toward a field that shares both its
problems and knowledge in dialogue among a wide community
of colleagues. Toward a *learning field* as much as an *educating
field*.

Is this a fantasy from a hopeless romantic? Perhaps. Perhaps nothing will ever change. Perhaps others will be writing
for yet another century wondering why we never could come
together with the technologies right at our fingertips. Perhaps
our field will always be at the margins of the educational, political, and professional worlds of our society, and we will never
be more than we are now. It is easy to become cynical in adult
literacy. But it is optimism, not cynicism, that brings our learners to programs. It is optimism, not cynicism, that keeps us going in this field. We are, more exactly, *"hopeful* romantics."
What we ultimately need, I think, are larger dreams and the
greater confidence needed to turn them into reality.

Jonathon Dale, a Quaker who has spent much of his life as a
community worker in some of England's most depressed inner-
cities once wrote: "First we must dream. Nothing is harder . . .
[since] dreaming has to break through the constantly reinforced
assumption that 'There is no alternative'" (1996, p. 1). In adult
literacy we have alternatives, but we rarely see them and often
do not act on them. With little or no sense of history, we have

come to think that the way this field now functions is somehow "normal," and that there are "no real alternatives." While it is a privilege and responsibility to help fulfill the dreams of our learners, we need to be able to say with professional pride: "There are indeed alternatives in this field of ours. Both for our learners and ourselves. And we will explore them together."

CHAPTER 5
ACTIVITIES YOU MIGHT CONSIDER

In this and earlier chapters, you have been referred to this section for ways to study and evaluate your own ideas for practice problems. To develop an action research study, you might begin by looking at some of the Websites listed in the Further Reading section on page 201 to ascertain what has been done on any question that is important to you and your program. First, here is a checklist to help you work through your own study question.

A CHECK LIST TO HELP PLAN AND
IMPLEMENT A STUDY

A. The Problem-Posing Phase

After bringing a few others together who have experience with this issue and/or who have an interest in your study as a research circle, discuss the following questions:

- What is "the itch?" The issue that seems to be coming up and which can't seem to be resolved through everyday attempts to do something about it? What are the various aspects of it? (Describe how you see it to your research circle colleagues.)
- Why do you think the problem exists? How do others involved depict it?
- What is the aspect of the problem that you want to address in this study? Can you state the question in one interrogative statement? Begin with terms like: "How," "Why," or "What if."

- Is this actually the problem you want to spend time on? Will others agree to help? Will the research circle agree to spend time helping with this? Are there prior studies on this very issue? (Search program Websites and research data bases such as ERIC.)
- Do you have any initial ideas on how to intervene to address this problem? State these and see if what others think.

B. The Planning Phase

- What new strategy or approach does the group agree might make a difference? What can you do differently? What is the **"best hunch"** for change?
- Describe the proposed intervention in general terms. Can you describe it in terms of a series of steps?
- What is your **timeline**? When will you begin? When will you stop? Explain these dates.
- Draw a flow chart with a sequence of steps. Be sure it is a study that allows you to manage the steps and observe the activities.
- What materials/equipment will you need? Why?
- Whose administrative approval will you need?
- How will you inform the participants and gain their consent? What will you do if a student does not want to participate?
- What will your **baseline** be for a point of comparison?
- What will the **criteria for success** be? What degree or percentage or statements or amount of change will be acceptable for success? Why these criteria?
- What **data collection techniques** will you use to collect the data (see list of examples)?
- What might discourage you from finishing this project? What barriers do you foresee? How can they be worked on now so they are not barriers later?

C. The Observation Phase

Having decided on your best **hunch**, a **timeline**, a **baseline**, the **criteria for success**, as well as your **data collection tech-**

niques, consider the logistics of putting the plan in place, keeping the following questions in mind:

- Are you staying true to the initial plan? Is action research the best approach?
- Are you collecting the data the way you said you would? Including a research journal? Do you have at least 3 collection techniques?
- Are you keeping in touch with your research circle for support in seeing the project through and confirming that the project is on track? Do you need to alter it?
- Develop a summary of what you thought occurred and how well the study went at the end of the timeline. This can be done in your research journal.

CHOOSING DATA COLLECTION TECHNIQUES

For an action research project, it is typically recommended you choose at least three of these techniques during the planning phase of the project:

Written Forms of Data Collection:

Research journals: These are invaluable for keeping an on-going, reflective record of events. Research journal entries are typically written at the end of a day or when there is relative calm after a passage of time. The research journal allows you to describe the events of the study and also to comment and reflect on events. They will also be most helpful at the end of a project when you look back and then can see patterns and changes which were not apparent at the time of the events. They are a useful reminder of what you were dealing with, and concerned with, at any given time during the study.

Anecdotal records: Anecdotal records are written accounts of observed details of events that occur during the study. They can go further to include what is called "thick description" of your observations of unspoken rules, routines, observed beliefs, and interchanges that characterize a given situation. Again, they can provide insights into patterns not obvious at the time of the entries.

Questionnaires: These are written sets of questions requiring written responses. There are basically of two types:

- **Open** involves asking for opinions and a considerable range of information in the participant's own words. These are especially useful for exploratory topics, but they can be hard to analyze. Open questionnaires are obviously of little value if the reading level is not high. All questionnaires should be pilot tested to be sure the language is clear before using them.
- **Closed** involves asking for direct written answers to questions with limited space provided for the answer or multiple choice. They seek concise answers to concise questions. Closed questionnaires can use a Likert scale, e.g., 1 to 5 or 1 to 7—where 1 is "strongly agree," and the highest number is "strongly disagree," similar to the inventory read aloud in chapter four.

Oral Forms of Data Collection:

If you are using an oral method of collecting data, it can be important to also have some means to record the data, either in the form of note taking or using a video and/or tape recorder. These oral accounts take various forms.

Interviews: Useful when the topic is emotionally charged, when in-depth reflection is to be involved, or when reading will be a problem, interviews can be carried out with groups or individuals. Interviews are often categorized into three types:

- **Structured.** This form does not seek discussion or interpretations; rather, direct responses are given. Useful when specific information is being sought.
- **Semi-structured.** This form begins each question with the same opening but goes further than the question with "probes,"

whereby the interviewer asks follow-up questions in pre-determined areas.

- **Open-ended** or Conversational. This form encourages a free-ranging discussion with minimal direction from the interviewer.

Focus Groups: Interviews are carried out with small groups and are typically focused on a particular theme. Used widely for marketing research, the benefit of a focus group is that participants can hear each others' responses and react accordingly. They can require considerable group process skills on the part of the interviewer to keep the discussion on track and to keep the group interaction balanced.

Document analysis: Involves reviewing/analyzing existing documentation such as past student attendance records, earlier evaluations, or grades.

D. The Reflection Phase

Having reassembled the research circle, look at the data collected. Analyze the data in pairs or individually, but cross-reference your conclusions on the patterns that have emerged to build trustworthiness and consistency in the triangulation of the data. Try asking the following questions:

- What do the data reveal about your problem and the interventions you tried?
- Were your criteria for success met? How far are you from attaining them?
- What were the tangible gains? What were the disappointments?
- What did not go as well as you planned? Why?
- How could you repeat this to enhance consistency and trustworthiness?
- Will you enter a second cycle of the project trying a more refined intervention? A third?

CHAPTER 5: FURTHER READING

Action Research

Kemmis, S., & McTaggart, R. (1988). *The action research planner* (3rd Ed.). Geelong, Australia: Deakin University Press.
Quigley, B. A., & Kuhne, G. (Eds.). (1997). *Creating practical knowledge through action research: Posing problems, solving problems, and improving daily practice.* New Directions for Adult and Continuing Education No. 73. San Francisco: Jossey-Bass.
Reason, P., & Bradbury, H. (Eds.). (2001). *Handbook of action research.* Thousand Oaks, CA: Sage.

Literacy Research Websites at Literacy Programs and Institutes

Australia
Adult Literacy and Numeracy Research Consortium (ALNARC)
www.staff.vu.edu.au/alnarc

National Center for English Language Teaching & Research (NCELTR)
www.nceltr.mq.edu.au/amep/index.html

Canada
Adult Literacy Research in Ontario
www.research.alphaplus.ca

Festival of Literacies, Ontario
www.literaciesoise.ca

National Adult Literacy Database
www.nald.ca

Nova Scotia Action Research Movement
www.ns.literacy.ca/nsarmove/resrchmv.htm

Research-in-Practice in Adult Literacy
www.nald.ca/ripal

The Directory of Canadian Adult Literacy Research in English
www.nald.ca/crd

England
Research & Practice in Adult Literacy
www.literacy.lancs.ac.uk/rapal

Lancaster Literacy Research Centre
www.literacy.lancaster.ac.uk/what/teachers.htm

United States of America
Kentucky Practitioner Inquiry Projects
www.workforce.ky.gov

National Centre for the Study of Adult Learning and Literacy
gseweb.harvard.edu/~ncsall/index.html

Pennsylvania Adult Literacy Practitioner Inquiry Network (PALPIN)
www.learningfrompractice.org/palpin/default.htm

Pennsylvania Action Research Network (PAARN)
http://www.pde.state.pa.us/able/cwp/view.asp?A=215&Q=110085

Project Idea, Texas
slincs.coe.utk.edu/research.htm

Virginia Adult Education Research Network (VAERN)
www.aelweb.vcu.edu/resguide/resguide1

Women Expanding / Literacy Education Action Resource Network
http://www.litwomen.org/welearn.html

CHAPTER 6

A Closing Note: Professional Development as "A State of Mind"

"I do not think anyone can seriously engage in a search for new knowledge without using his or her point of view and historical location as a point of departure."

—P. Freire, 1985

Looking back for a moment, I'd like to ask: "Have you ever looked in a photo album and seen a photo of yourself taken a few years ago?" And then said: "Have I ever changed!" After thinking about your life back then, (and getting past the grim facts of aging), you thought to yourself: "If I only knew then what I know now." I am hoping this might be the point where you now find yourself on your professional development journey. You know more now than you did at the outset (and have not aged too much as a result of the experience, I hope).

You and your friends began by opening your learning journals and by joining a learning circle—later a research circle. Now, some time later, the opening thoughts you had to the *very first set of questions* are of special interest. How would you answer those Chapter 1 first questions now? What did you say back then? Any changes? What about the other opening and learning circle questions? What about changes you see in your entries in your journal? Maybe, in some instances, what you knew before is basically the same now, but has it been reinforced? Maybe you have a better sense of why you thought that then—

and now. Or you have a better framework for what you thought before. Or perhaps you have been challenged to think in new ways and try new ideas. These are the keys to that "state of mind" that makes us more professional.

Start From Where You Are

As noted along the way in this guide, the structure of this book was *not* to start with learners, nor with funding agencies, nor with policy makers, nor even to begin to list out the "gaps in knowledge or skills" that needed to be filled before assuming to be a profession. This professional development program began with you and ended with you. We began with some questions about professionalism and considered some professionalism issues. We moved to exemplary historical heroes and then directly to you. Only after consideration of ourselves and our place in this larger field did we come to our learners, and only *then* did we move to the teaching process. Indeed, this was the same logic in the intake and model course in Chapter 4—*begin with where the learners are; the rest will follow if we trust in them.* It was only in the final chapter that problem solving and action research were discussed. From yourself, to your learners, and then to *your* issues. Why begin and end with you? This professional development program was intended to be about you because it is the practitioners—first and last—who keep this field alive. It is the dedicated teachers, tutors and administrators who keep the momentum going. The journey is not over. It is just beginning.

What Did We Talk About?

Let's think back. What did we talk about? First it was about the very concept of professionalism and "A Way Forward" with a praxis model. Questions were raised about the notions of professionalism—pros and cons of certification and how your own program was functioning. Then we discussed the courage and fortitude of some of our literacy heroes and heroines through time. There was a chance to build greater pride in the rich history of our field, including a chance "to think *and* act locally" with an activity to research your own program's history. We then looked at practice philosophies and had a chance to reflect on "what I believe" and "why I teach." We considered other "ways of seeing" in adult education, and options we have for thinking about literacy practice.

We moved on in Chapter 3 to look at some principles of adult learning, especially as they relate to adults with low literacy skills. We considered some of the barriers that confront our learners along with some ideas on how to address those barriers. We had a model intake and program to think about. There may have been some ideas in that chapter that could be adapted or adopted in your daily program. Lastly, we got a chance to think about a way to develop systematic knowledge through action research as we seek to solve the unique problems we so often face in our practice. But maybe they are not so unique after all. The proposal made in the closing pages was to share problems and promising solutions electronically, and in other ways—to teach in a more interdependent way, and learn in a more interdependent way.

Where to From Here?

We began noting the strength of caring and compassion in this field. The heart, the hand, and the head were all discussed, with the heart seen as the "first among equal parts." I'd like to end where this began—with values, and my favorite quote on values. It is by philosopher and theologian Reinhold Neibuhr:

> Nothing that is worth doing can be [fully] achieved in our lifetime; therefore we must be saved by hope. Nothing which is true or beautiful or good makes complete sense in any immediate context of history; therefore, we must be saved by faith. Nothing we do, however virtuous, can be accomplished alone; therefore we must be saved by love. (1952, p. 63).

REFERENCES

Akenson, J. E., & Neufeldt, H. G. (1990). The Southern literacy campaign for Black adults in the early twentieth century. In H. G. Neufeldt, & L. McGee (Eds.), *Education of the African American adult*, pp. 179–190). Westport, CT: Greenwood Press.

Alexander, A. (1997). *The Antigonish movement: Moses Coady and adult education today*. Toronto: Thompson Educational Publishing.

American Missionary Association (1868). *22nd Annual report*. American Missionary Archives, Amistad Research Center, New Orleans: Author.

Argyris, C. (1989). *Reasoning, learning, and action: Individual and organizational*. San Francisco: Jossey-Bass.

Argyris, C., Putnam, R., & McLain Smith, D. (1985) *Action science: Concepts, methods, and skills for research and intervention*, San Francisco: Jossey-Bass.

Arnove, R. F., & Graff, H. J. (1987). *National literacy campaigns: Historical and comparative perspectives*. New York: Plenum Press.

Aslanian, C. B., & Brickell, H. M. (1980). *Americans in transition: Life changes as reasons for adult learning*. New York: College Entrance Examination Board.

Ausubel, D. P. (1968). *Educational psychology: A cognitive view*. New York: Holt, Rinehart & Winston.

Baldwin, Y. H. (2005). *Cora Wilson Stewart and the Moonlight Schools: Fighting for literacy in Kentucky*. Lexington: University Press of Kentucky.

Barr, J. (1999). Women, adult education and really useful knowledge. In J. Crowther, I. Martin & M. Shaw, (Eds.), *Popular education and social movements in Scotland today*. Leiscester, UK: NIACE.

Beder, H. (1989). Purposes and philosophies of adult education. In S. Merriam & P. Cunningham (Eds.), *Handbook of adult and continuing education*, pp. 37–50. San Francisco: Jossey-Bass.

Beder, H. (1994). The current status of adult literacy education in the United States. *PAACE Journal of Lifelong Learning, 3*, 14–25.

Bee, H. L. (1992). *The journey of adulthood* (3rd ed.). Toronto: Macmillan Canada.

Bee, H. L. (2000). *The journey of adulthood* (4th ed.). Toronto: Macmillan Canada.

Belfiore, M., & Folinsbee, S. (2000). A collaborative committee process in the workplace. In P. Campbell & B. Burnaby (Eds.), *Participatory practices in adult education,* pp. 167–184. Mahwah, NJ: Lawrence Erlbaum.

Bell, B., Gaventa, J., & Peters, J. (1990). *We make the road by walking: Conversations on education and social changes.* Philadelphia: Temple University Press.

Belzer, A. (2005). Improving professional development systems: Recommendations from the Pennsylvania adult basic and literacy education professional development system evaluation. *Adult Basic Education, 1*(15), 33–55.

Belzer, A., & St. Clair, R. (2003). *Opportunities and limits: An update on adult literacy education,* (Information Series No. 391). Columbus, OH: ERIC.

Berton, P. (1988). *The Arctic grail: The quest for the North West passage and the North Pole. 1818–1909.* Toronto: McClelland & Stewart.

Benseman, J. (2001). *Making learning happen.* Wellington, NZ: Skill New Zealand—Pūkenga Aotearoa.

Billington, R. A. (1953). Introduction. In R. A. Billington (Ed.), *The Journal of Charlotte Forten* (Rev. ed.), pp. 7–42. New York: W. W. Norton.

Blakely, R. (1957). The path and the goal. *Adult Education, 7*(2), 93–98.

Brookfield, S. D. (1988). *Developing critical thinkers.* San Francisco: Jossey-Bass.

Brookfield, S. D. (1990). *The skillful teacher.* San Francisco: Jossey-Bass.

Brookfield, S. D. (1991). Using critical incidents to explore learners' assumptions. In J. Mezirow & Assoc. (Eds.). *Fostering critical reflection in adulthood,* San Francisco: Jossey-Bass.

Brookfield, S. D. (1995). *Becoming a critically reflective teacher.* San Francisco: Jossey-Bass.

Brookfield, S. D. (1998). Understanding and facilitating moral learning in adults. *Journal of Moral Education, 7*(3), 283–296.

Bruner, J. (1965). In defense of verbal learning. In R. C. Anderson

& D. P. Ausubel (Eds.), *Readings in the psychology of cognition*, pp. 87–102. New York: Holt, Rinehart & Winston.

Bryan, M., Bair, B., & DeAngury, M. (2003). *The selected papers of Jane Addams*, Vol. 1. Chicago: University of Illinois Press.

Burnaford, G., Fischer, J., & Hobson, D. (2001). *Teachers doing research*. (2nd ed.). Mahwah, NJ: Lawrence Erlbaum.

Button, H. W., & Provenzo, E. F. (1983). *History of education and culture in America*. Englewood Cliffs, NJ: Prentice Hall.

By the light of the moon, shy Kentuckians were taught to read. (2001, October). *The Kentucky Explorer*, pp. 10–12.

Caffarella, R. S. (1994). *Planning programs for adult learners*. San Francisco: Jossey-Bass.

Campbell, P. (2001). Introduction. In P. Campbell & B. Burnaby (Eds.), *Participatory practices in adult education*, pp. 1–14. Mahwah, NJ: Lawrence Erlbaum.

Campbell. P., &. Burnaby, B. (Eds.), (2001). *Participatory practices in adult education*, Mahwah, NJ: Lawrence Erlbaum.

Cervero, R. M. (1988). *Effective continuing education for professionals*. San Francisco: Jossey-Bass.

Cervero, R. M., & Wilson, A. L. (1994). *Planning responsibly for adult education: A guide to negotiating interests and power*. San Francisco: Jossey-Bass.

Cervero, R. M, & Wilson, A. L., & Associates (Eds.). (2001). *Power in practice: Adult education and the struggle for knowledge and power in society*. San Francisco: Jossey-Bass.

Chisman, F. P. & Associates (1990). *Leadership for Literacy*. San Francisco: Jossey-Bass.

Coady, M. M. (1939). *Masters of their own destiny*. New York: Harper and Brothers.

Cochran-Smith, M., & Lytle, S. (1993). *Inside/outside: Teacher research and knowledge*. New York: Teacher College Press.

Collins, M. (1983). A critical analysis of competency-based systems in adult education. *Adult Education Quarterly, 3*(33), 174–182.

Collins, M. (1987). *Competence in adult education: A new perspective*. Lanham, MD: University Press of America.

Collins, M. (1991). *Adult education as vocation: A critical role for the adult educator*. New York: Routledge.

Comings, J. P. (2003, September). *Establishing an evidence-based adult education system*. NCSALL occasional paper.

Cook, W. D. (1977). *Adult literacy education in the United States*. Newark, DE: International Reading Association.

Covey, S. R. (1990). *The seven habits of highly effective people.* New York: Simon & Schuster.

Cranton, P. (2003). *Finding our way.* Dayton, OH: Wall & Emerson.

Cremin, L. A. (1961). *The transformation of the school: Progressivism in American education.* New York: Vintage Books.

Cronbach, L. J. (1980). *Toward reform of program evaluation.* San Francisco: Jossey-Bass.

Cross, K. P. (1982). *Adults as learners.* San Francisco: Jossey-Bass.

Crowther, J., Hamilton, M., & Tett, L. (Eds.), (2001). *Powerful literacies.* Leicester, England: NIACE.

Cunningham, P. (1989). Making a more significant impact in society. In A. Quigley (Ed.), *Fulfilling the promise of adult and continuing education,* pp. 33–46. New Directions for Continuing Education, no. 44. San Francisco: Jossey-Bass.

Dale, J. (1996). *Beyond the spirit of the age.* London: Quaker Home Service.

Darkenwald, G. G., & Merriam, S. B. (1982). *Adult Education: Foundations of practice.* New York: Harper & Row.

Davidson, H. (2001). Possibilities for participatory practice through prisoners' own educational practices. In P. Campbell & B. Burnaby (Eds.), *Participatory practices in adult education,* pp. 237–266. Mahwah, NJ: Lawrence Erlbaum.

Davis, A. F. (1973). *American heroine: The life and legend of Jane Addams.* New York: Oxford University Press.

DeBoer, C. M. (1995). *His truth is marching on: African Americans who taught the freed men for the American Missionary Association, 1861–1877.* New York: Garland Publishing.

Demetrion, G. (2005). *Conflicting paradigms in adult literacy education: In quest of a U.S. democratic politics of literacy.* Mahwah, NJ: Lawrence Erlbaum.

Diliberto, G. (1999). *A useful woman: The early life of Jane Addams.* New York: Scribner's.

Dirkx, J., & Prenger, S. (1997), *A guide for planning and implementing instruction for Adults.* San Francisco: Jossey-Bass.

Draper, J. A. (1989). A historical view of literacy. In M. C. Taylor & J. A. Draper (Eds.), *Adult literacy perspectives,* pp. 71–80. Toronto: Culture Concepts.

Elias, J. L., & Merriam, S. B. (2005). Philosophical foundations of adult education (3rd ed.). San Francisco: Jossey-Bass.

English, L. M., & Gillen, M. A. (2001). *Promoting journal writing in adult education.* New Directions for Adult and Continuing Education, no. 90. San Francisco: Jossey-Bass.

Erskine, J. (1943). *The complete life*. New York: J. Messer.

Estes, F. (1988). *Cora Wilson Stewart and the moonlight schools Kentucky, 1911–1920. A case study in the rhetorical uses of literacy*. Unpublished doctoral dissertation, University of Kentucky, Lexington.

Ewing, G. (2003, Spring) The new literacies studies. *Literacies (1)*, 15–19.

Fernandes, W., & Tandon, R. (1981). *Participatory research and evaluation*. New Delhi: Aruna Printing Press.

Ferris, H. (1943). *When I was a girl: The stories of five famous women told by themselves*. New York: Macmillan.

Fetterman, D. (1997). Case Studies of action research in various adult education settings. In B. A. Quigley & G. Kuhne, G. (Eds.). *Creating practical knowledge through action research: Posing problems, solving problems, and improving daily practice*, pp. 41–62. New Directions for Adult and Continuing Education, no. 73. San Francisco: Jossey-Bass.

Fingeret, A. (1983). Social network: A new perspective on independence and illiterate adults. *Adult Education Quarterly, 33*(3), 133–146.

Fingeret, H. A. (1989). The social and historical context of participatory literacy education. In H. A. Fingeret & P. Jurmo (Eds.), *Participatory literacy education*. New Directions for Continuing Education, no. 42. San Francisco: Jossey-Bass.

Fingeret, H., & Danin, S. (1991). *"They really put a hurtin' on my brain": Learning in literacy volunteers of New York*. Durham, NC: Literacy South.

Fingeret, H. A., & Jurmo, P. (1989). *Participatory literacy education*. New Directions for Continuing Education, no. 42. San Francisco: Jossey-Bass.

Firestone, W. A. (1987). Meaning in method: The rhetoric of quantitative and qualitative research. *Educational Researcher, 16*(7), 16–21.

Fischer, S. R. (2003). *A history of reading*. London: Reaktion Books.

Flecha, R. (2000). *Sharing words: Theory and practice of dialogic learning*. New York: Rowman & Littlefield.

Fleming, F. (1998). *Barrow's boys*. New York: Atlantic Monthly Press.

Flexner, A. (1910). *Medical Education in United States and Canada*. Boston: Merrymount Press.

Flexner, A. (1915). Is social work a profession? *School and Society*, 1, 901–911.

Foster, S. E. (1990). Upgrading the skills of literacy professionals: The profession matures. In F. P. Chisman & Associates (Eds.), *Leadership for literacy: The agenda for the 1990s*, pp. 73–94. San Francisco: Jossey-Bass.

Freire, P. (1973). *Pedagogy of the oppressed.* New York: Seabury Press.

Gage, N. L. (1989). The paradigm wars and their aftermath. *Educational Researcher, 18*(7), 4–10.

Galbraith, M., & Zelenak, B. (1989). The education of adult and continuing education practitioners. In S. Merriam & P. Cunningham (Eds.). *Handbook of adult and continuing education*, (pp. 124–167). San Francisco: Jossey-Bass.

Gillette, G. (1998). *Breaking the barriers: Fostering reflection on experience in a prison setting.* Unpublished master's thesis. St. Francis Xavier University, Antigonish, Nova Scotia.

Gilley, J. W., & Galbraith, M. W. (1992). Commonalities and characteristics of professional certification: Implications for adult education. *Lifelong learning: An Omnibus of Practice and Research, 12*(1), 11–14, 17.

Gowen, S. (1992). *The politics of workplace literacy: A case study.* New York: Teachers College Press.

Grattan, H. C. (1955). *In quest of knowledge: A historical perspective on adult education.* New York: Association Press.

Grattan, H. C. (Ed.). (1959). *American ideas about Adult education: 1710–1951.* New York: Teachers College Press.

Griffith, W. S., & Cervero, R. M. (1977). The adult performance level program: A serious and deliberate examination. *Adult Education, 27*, 209–224.

Guba, E. G., & Lincoln, Y. S. (1988). *Effective evaluation.* San Francisco: Jossey-Bass.

Hall, B. L. (2001). I wish this were a poem of practices of participatory research. In P. Reason & H. Bradbury, (Eds.). (2002). *Handbook of action research*, 171–178. Thousand Oaks, CA: Sage.

Haug, M. R. (1975). The deprofessionalization of everyone? *Sociological Focus, 8,* (197–213).

Heron, J. (1999). *The complete facilitator's handbook.* Sterling, VA: Kogan Page.

Hiemstra, R., & Sisco, B. (1990). *Individualizing Instruction.* San Francisco: Jossey-Bass.

Hirsh, E. (1988). *Cultural literacy: What every American needs to know.* New York: Random House.

hooks, b. (1994). *Teaching to transgress.* New York: Routledge.

Horsman, J. (1999). *Too scared to learn: Women, violence and education.* Toronto: McGilligan Books.

Houle, C. O. (1980). *Continuing learning in the professions.* San Francisco: Jossey-Bass.

Hudson, J. W. (1969). *The history of adult education.* London: Woburn Press. (Original work published 1851)

Hurston, Z. N. (1942). *Dust tracks on a road.* Philadelphia: J. B. Lippincott.

Illich, I. (1977). *Disabling professions.* New York: Marion Boyers Publishers.

James, W. B. (1992). Professional certification is not needed in adult and continuing education. In M. Galbraith & B. Sisco (Eds.), *Confronting controversies in challenging times: A call for action* (pp. 125–131). New Directions for Adult and Continuing Education, no. 54. San Francisco: Jossey-Bass.

James, W. B. (1989). Certification is unfeasible and unnecessary. In B. W. Krietlow (Ed.), *Examining controversies in adult education* (pp. 84–96). San Francisco: Jossey-Bass.

Jarvis, P. (1990). *An international dictionary of adult and continuing education.* London: Routledge.

Jarvis, P. (1999). *The practitioner-researcher: Developing theory from practice.* San Francisco: Jossey-Bass.

Jurmo, P. (1989a). The case for participatory literacy education. In H. A. Fingeret & P. Jurmo (Eds.), *Participatory literacy education,* pp. 17–28. New Directions for Adult and Continuing Education, no. 42. San Francisco: Jossey-Bass.

Jurmo, P. (1989b). Instruction and management: Where participation theory is put into practice. In A. Fingeret & P. Jurmo (Eds.), *Participatory literacy education,* pp. 29–34. New Directions for Adult and Continuing Education, no. 42. San Francisco: Jossey-Bass.

Kelly, T. (1962). *A history of adult education in Great Britain.* Liverpool, UK: Liverpool University Press.

Kemmis, S. (1990). Improving education through action research. In O. Zuber-Skerritt (Ed.), *Action research for change and development,* (pp. 79–100). Brisbane, Australia: Centre for Advancement and Teaching.

Kemmis, S., & McTaggart, R. (1988). *The action research planner* (3rd ed.). Geelong, Australia: Deakin University Press.

Kim, K., Collins-Hagedorn, M., & Williamson, J. (2004). *Participation in adult education and lifelong learning: 2000–01.* (NCES 2004-050). U.S. Department of Education, National Leader of Education Statistics. Washington, DC: Government Printing Office.

Kirsch, I., Jungeblut, A., Jenkins, L., & Kolstad, A. (1993). *Adult lit-*

eracy in America: A first look at the results of the national adult literacy survey. Washington, DC: U.S. Department of Education.

Kitchner, K., & King, P. M. (1990). The reflective judgement model: Transforming assumptions about knowing. In J. Mezirow & Assoc. (Eds.), *Fostering critical reflection in adulthood*, (pp. 159–176). San Francisco: Jossey-Bass.

Knowles, M. S. (1975). *Self-directed learning: A guide for learners and teachers*. Chicago: Gollett.

Knowles, M. S. (1980). *The modern practice of adult education*. New York: Cambridge.

Knowles, M. S. & Associates (1985). *Andragogy in action*. San Francisco: Jossey-Bass.

Knox, A. B. (1977). *Adult development and learning*. San Francisco: Jossey-Bass.

Koloski, J. A. (1989). Enhancing the field's image through professionalism and practice. In B. A. Quigley (Ed.), In *Fulfilling the promise of adult and continuing education* (pp. 71–78). New Directions for Adult and Continuing Education, no. 54. San Francisco: Jossey-Bass.

Krotz, L. (Ed.).(1999). *Frontier College letters: One hundred years of teaching, learning & nation building*. Toronto: Frontier College Press.

Lagemann, E. C. (Ed.). (1985). *Jane Addams on education*. New York: Teachers College Press.

Lander, D. A. (1996, August). The campus transgressions of the cook, the poet, and the philosopher. In M. Bal & M. Caro (Eds.), *Proceedings of the International Conference of Semiotics, territoriality and desire*, pp. 41–43, University of Amsterdam.

Lewin, K. (1946). Action research and minority issues. *Journal of Social Issues, 2*, 34–46.

Leypoldt, M. (1967) *40 ways to teach in groups*. Valley Forge, PA: Judson Press.

Linn, J. W. (1935). *Jane Addams: A biography*. New York: D. Appleton-Century.

Little, W., et al. (1970). *The shorter Oxford English dictionary* (3rd ed.). London: Oxford University Press.

Long, H. B. (1990). Understanding adult learners. In *Adult learning methods*. Malabar, FL: Krieger.

Lotz, J. (2005). *The humble giant: Moses Coady, Canada's rural revolutionary*. Ottawa, Canada: Novalis.

Lovett, B. L. (1990). Black adult education during the Civil War, 1861–1865. In H. Neufeldt & L. McGee (Eds.), *Education of the*

African American adult: An historical overview. Westport, CT: Greenwood Press.

Luttrell, W. (1996). Becoming somebody in and against school: Toward a psychocultural theory of gender and self making. In B. Levinson. D. Foley, & D. Holland (Eds.), *The cultural production of the educated person*. New York: State University of New York Press.

Lytle, S., & Cochran-Smith, M. (1990). Learning from teacher research: A working typology. *Teachers College Record, 92*(1), pp. 83–103.

Mandrell, L. (n.d.). *Eradicating illiteracy*. Morehead, KY: Morehead-Rowan County Chamber of Commerce.

Manguel, A. (1996). *A history of reading*. Toronto: Viking.

Martin, C. (1924). *The adult school movement*. London: National Adult School Union.

Mattran, K. J. (1989). Mandatory education increases professional competence. In B. W. Kreitlow (Ed.), *Examining controversies in adult education* (pp. 46–51). San Francisco: Jossey-Bass.

McDonald, K. S., & Wood, G. S. (1993). Surveying adult education practitioners about ethical issues. *Adult Education Quarterly, 43*(4), 243–257.

McKnight, J. (1977). The professional service business. *Social Policy, 8*, (110–116).

Merriam, S. B. (1991). How research produces knowledge. In J. M. Peters & P. Jarvis (Eds.), *Adult Education: Evolution and achievements in a developing field of study* (pp. 42–65). San Francisco: Jossey-Bass.

Merriam, S., & Brockett, R. (1997). *The profession and practice of adult education*. San Francisco: Jossey-Bass.

Merriam, S. B. & Caffarella, R. S. (1999). *Learning in Adulthood: A comprehensive guide*. San Francisco: Jossey-Bass.

Merriam, S. B., & Caffarella, R. S. (2005). Learning in adulthood: A comprehensive guide (2nd ed.). San Francisco: Jossey-Bass.

Merriam, S. B., & Simpson, E. L. (2000). *A guide to research for educators and trainers of adults* (2nd ed.). (updated). San Francisco: Jossey-Bass.

Merrifield, J. (1998). *Contested Ground: Performance Accountability in Adult Basic Education* (NCSALL Reports #1). Harvard University Graduate School of Education: National Centre for the Study of Adult Learning and Literacy (NCSALL).

Mezirow, J. (1991a). *Fostering critical reflection in adulthood: A guide to transformative and emancipatory learning*. San Francisco: Jossey-Bass.

Mezirow, J. (1991b). *Transformative dimensions of adult learning.* San Francisco: Jossey-Bass.

Mocker, D. W. (1974). *A report on the identification, classification, and rank of competencies appropriate for adult basic education in teachers.* Kansas City: University of Missouri.

Moore, L. (1997). *The thieves' opera.* New York: Harcourt Brace.

Morrison, J. H. (1989). *Camps & classrooms: A pictorial history of Frontier College.* Toronto: Frontier College Press.

Neibuhr, R. (1952). *The irony of American history.* Scribner's.

Niks, N., Allen, D. Davies, P., MacRae, D. & Nonesuch, K. (2003). *Dancing in the dark: How do adults with little formal education learn?* Duncan, BC: Canada: Malaspina University Press.

Norton, M. (2001). Getting our own education: Peer tutoring and participatory education in an adult literacy centre. In P. Campbell & B. Burnaby (Eds.), *Participatory practices in adult education,* pp. 103–122. Mahwah, NJ: Lawrence Erlbaum.

Norton, M., & Malicky, G. (2000). *Learning about participatory approaches in adult literacy education.* Six research in practice studies. Edmonton, Alberta: Learning at the Centre Press.

Organization for Economic Co-operation and Development (OECD), and Statistics Canada (2000). *Literacy in the information age.* Ottawa: Government of Canada.

Ouzts, D. T. (1991). The Emergence of Bibliotherapy as a Discipline. *Reading Horizons, 31*(3), 199–206.

Patton, M. Q. (1987). *How to use qualitative methods in evaluation.* Newbury Park, CA: Sage.

Peers, R. (1972). *Adult education: A comparative study.* New York: Humanities Press.

Pratt, D. D. (1988). Andragogy as a rational construct. *Adult Education Quarterly, 38*(3), 160–181.

Queeney, D. S., & English, J. K. (1994). *Mandatory continuing education: A status report.* Columbus, OH: ERIC.

Quigley, B. A. (1987). *The resisters: An analysis of non-participation in adult basic education.* Unpublished doctoral dissertation, Northern Illinois University, De Kalb.

Quigley, B. A. (1997). *Rethinking adult education: The critical need for practice-based change.* San Francisco: Jossey-Bass.

Quigley, B. A. (1998). The first three weeks: Critical time for motivation. *Focus on Basics, 2,* pp. 6–11.

Quigley, B. A. (2001). Living in the feudalism of adult basic and literacy education: Can we negotiate a literacy democracy? In C. A. Hansman & P. A. Sissel (Eds.), *Understanding and negotiating the political landscape of adult education*, pp. 55–62. New Directions for Adult and Continuing Education, No. 91. San Francisco: Jossey-Bass.

Quigley, B. A. (2005). Literacy. In L. M. English (Ed.), *The International encyclopaedia of adult education*, pp. 381–387). New York: Palgrave Macmillan.

Quigley, B. A., & Holsinger, E. (1993). Happy consciousness: Ideology and hidden curricula in literacy education. *Adult Education Quarterly, 44*(1), 17–33.

Quigley, B. A., & Kuhne, G. (Eds.). (1997). *Creating practical knowledge through action research: Posing problems, solving problems, and improving daily practice.* New Directions for Adult and Continuing Education, no. 73. San Francisco: Jossey-Bass.

Quigley, B. A., & Norton, M. (2002). *It simply makes us better: Learning from literacy research in practice networks in the UK, Australia and the United States.* Edmonton, AB: The Learning Centre.

Quigley, B. A., & Uhland, R. (2000). Retaining adult learners in the first three critical weeks: A Quasi-experimental model for ABLE programs. *Adult Basic Education, 10*(2), 55–68.

Quigley, B. A., & Watkins, K. E. (2001). Poking and prying with purpose. *Adult Learning, 11*(3), 3–5.

Rachal, J. R. (1986). Freedom's crucible: William T. Richardson and the schooling of freed men. *Adult Education Quarterly, 1*(37), 14–22.

Reason, P., & Bradbury, H. (Eds.). (2001). *Handbook of action research.* Thousand Oaks, CA: Sage.

Reder, S. M., & Green, K. R. (1985). *Giving literacy away,* Portland, OR: Literacy and language program, Northwest Regional Laboratory.

Riordan, R. J., & Wilson, L. S. (1989). Bibliotherapy: Does It Work? *Journal of Counseling and Development, 67*(9). [EJ 396 292].

Rogers, C. R. (1983). Freedom to learn for the 80s. Columbus, OH: Merrill Publishing.

Rose, A.D. (2001). Differing modes of inquiry and the field of adult education. *Adult Learning, 11*(3), 23–24.

Rosenkranz Cameron, C. (1989). Certification should be established. In *Examining controversies in adult education*, pp. 84–96. San Francisco: Jossey-Bass.

Rubenson, K. (1989). Sociology of adult education. In S. B. Merriam & P. M. Cunningham (Eds.), *Handbook of adult and continuing education*, pp. 51–69. San Francisco: Jossey-Bass.

Sabatini, J. P., Ginsberg, L., & Russell, M. (2002). Professionalization and certification for teachers of adult basic education. In J. Comings,

B. Garner, & C. Smith (Eds.), *Annual review of adult learning and literacy* (Vol. 3). Cambridge, MA: National Center for the Study of Adult Learning and Literacy.

Schön, D. A. (1983). *The reflective practitioner.* New York: Basic Books.

Selman, G., Selman, M., Cooke, M., & Dampier, P. (1998). *The foundations of adult education in Canada* (2nd ed.). Toronto: Thompson Educational Publishing.

Silberman, M. (1990). *Active training: A handbook of techniques, designs, case examples, and tips.* NY: Maxwell Macmillan International.

Smith, D. H. (1978, Winter). The determination of necessary competencies for adult basic education teachers. *Adult Literacy and Basic Education,* 47–56.

Smith, E. (1977). Introduction. In W. D. Cook, *Adult literacy education in the United States.* Newark, DE: International Reading Association.

Smith, C., & Hofer, J. (2003, November). *The characteristics and concerns of adult basic education teachers.* NCSALL Reports #26., Cambridge, MA: Harvard Graduate School of Education.

Smith, C., & Hofer, J. (2002). Pathways to change: A summary of the findings from NCSALL's staff development study. *Focus on Basics, 5* (D), 1, 3–7.

Smith, J. K., & Heshusius, L. (1986). Closing down the conversation: The end of the quantitative-qualitative debate. *Educational Researcher, 15*(1), 4–13.

Sork, T., & Welock, B. A. (1992). Adult education needs a code of ethics. In M. W. Galbraith & B. R. Sisco (Eds.), *Confronting controversies in challenging times: A call for action.* (pp. 115–122). New Directions for Adult and Continuing Education, No. 54 San Francisco: Jossey-Bass.

Sticht, T. G. (2002). The rise of the adult education and literacy system in the United States: 1600–2000. In J. Coming, B. Garner, & C. Smith (Eds.), *Annual review of adult learning and literacy* (Vol. 3, pp. 10–43). San Francisco: Jossey-Bass.

Stubblefield, H. (2002). Forging a new mission: Implications from the experiences of antecedent national associations. *Adult Learning, 13*(4), 4–6.

Stubblefield, H. W., & Keane, P. (1994). *Adult education in the American experience.* San Francisco: Jossey-Bass.

Swint, H. L. (1967). *The Northern teacher in the South: 1862–1870.* New York: Octagon Press.

Taylor, A. P. (1973). *Cora Wilson Stewart: Adult education, and edu-*

cational odyssey. Unpublished doctoral dissertation, Morehead State University, Morehead, KY.

Thomas, A. M., Taylor, M. C., & Gaskin, C. (Eds.). (1981). Federal legislation and adult basic education in Canada. In *Adult literacy perspectives*, pp. 41–56. Toronto: Culture Concepts.

T'Kenye, C. (1998). The nurturing perspective: Facilitating self-efficacy. In D. D. Pratt & Associates, (Ed.), *Five perspectives on teaching in adult and higher education*, pp. 151–172. Malabar, FL: Krieger.

Vella, J. (1994). *Learning to listen, learning to teach*. San Francisco: Jossey-Bass.

Verner, C. (1967). *Pole's history of adult schools*. Washington, DC: Adult Education Associates of the U.S.A. (Original work published, 1812)

Vidich, A. J., & Lyman, S. M. (2000). Qualitative methods: Their history in sociology and anthropology. In N. K. Denzin & Y. S. Lincoln (Eds.), *Handbook of Qualitative research* (2nd ed.), pp. 78–84. Thousand Oaks, CA: Sage.

Welton, M. R. (2001). *Little Mosie from the Margaree: A biography of Moses Michael Coady*. Toronto: Thompson Education Publishing.

Williamson, P. B. (2001). *The social construction of literacy*. Unpublished doctoral dissertation, University of Sydney, Australia.

Witkin, H. A., Oitman, P. K., Raskin, E., & Karp, S. A. (1971). *A manual for the embedded figures test*. Palo Alto, CA: Consulting Psychologist Press.

Wlodlowski, R. (1999). *Enhancing adult motivation to learn*. San Francisco: Jossey-Bass.

Wlodlowski, R. J. (1988). *Enhancing adult motivation to learn*. San Francisco: Jossey-Bass.

Zacharakis-Jutz, J. (2001). Strategic planning in rural town meetings: Issues related to citizen participation and democratic decision making. In P. Campbell & B. Burnaby (Eds.), *Participatory practices in adult education*, pp. 143–166. Mahwah, NJ: Lawrence Erlbaum.

Zeichner, K. (2001). Educational action research. In P. Reason & H. Bradbury (Eds.), *Handbook of action research: Participative inquiry and practice*, pp. 273–283. Thousand Oaks, CA: Sage.

INDEX